The Recyclosaurus and EggBangers

In memory of Emee-Lou

The Recyclosaurus and EggBangers

by

A R Trent

Illustrated by A R Trent

Characters – Robby and Nay Rabbit inspired by Lanayah Alyssa Williams,

(Lanayah the Book Slayer) aged 6

YOUCAXTON
PUBLICATIONS

Copyright © A R Trent 2025

The Author asserts the moral right to
be identified as the author of this work.

ISBN 978-1-915972-63-7
Published by YouCaxton Publications 2025

All rights reserved. No part of this publication may be reproduced, stored in a retrieval system, or transmitted in any form or by any means, electronic, mechanical, photocopying, recording or otherwise, without the prior permission of the author.

This book is sold subject to the condition that it shall not, by way of trade or otherwise, be lent, resold, hired out or otherwise circulated without the author's prior consent in any form of binding or cover other than that in which it is published and without a similar condition including this condition being imposed on the subsequent purchaser.

YouCaxton Publications
www.youcaxton.co.uk

Contents

LA-LA Forest Park	1
Well, isn't it winter?	1
THE RECYCLOSAURUS AND EGGBANGERS	4
NO SCHOOL TODAY	7
EMEE'S DOGNAPPED STORY	12
LITTLE BRO MEETS ED	20
BIZZY AND BIONCA	27
SCOTTY AND BIG BRO	32
GREG'S PLAN-B BAG	40
HOMELESS MASCULUS!	49
DUCKY'S TIN POT TRAP!	53
FROGLIP'S METAL LILYPOND	56
MISSRED OCEAN TURTLE OIL-SLICK!	58
STAG'S FOSSIL FUEL FARTS	59
THE SEAGULLS	66
NASTY PATSY	70
MAGPIE TURBO POOPS!	78

THE RECYCLOSAURUS	83
HANDSOME THE OWL	86
BLUTE BIRD SCIENTIST	91
ED THE GUILTY SUPER-DUPER POLLUTER!	110
ED'S UNBORN MESSAGE	117
A CAULDRON SPELL FOR NITTY NORA	124
THE BIRD WALK PAGEANT	127
BENEATH THE OASIS	132
OCEAN CRYSTAL CAVES	140
THE SPRINGUSAURUS	147
SECRET GARDEN FEAST	152
CASTLE HUT DINER	157
THE RETURN OF THE DOG CATCHER!	161
PROFESSOR MICROCHIP CONCLUDES	166

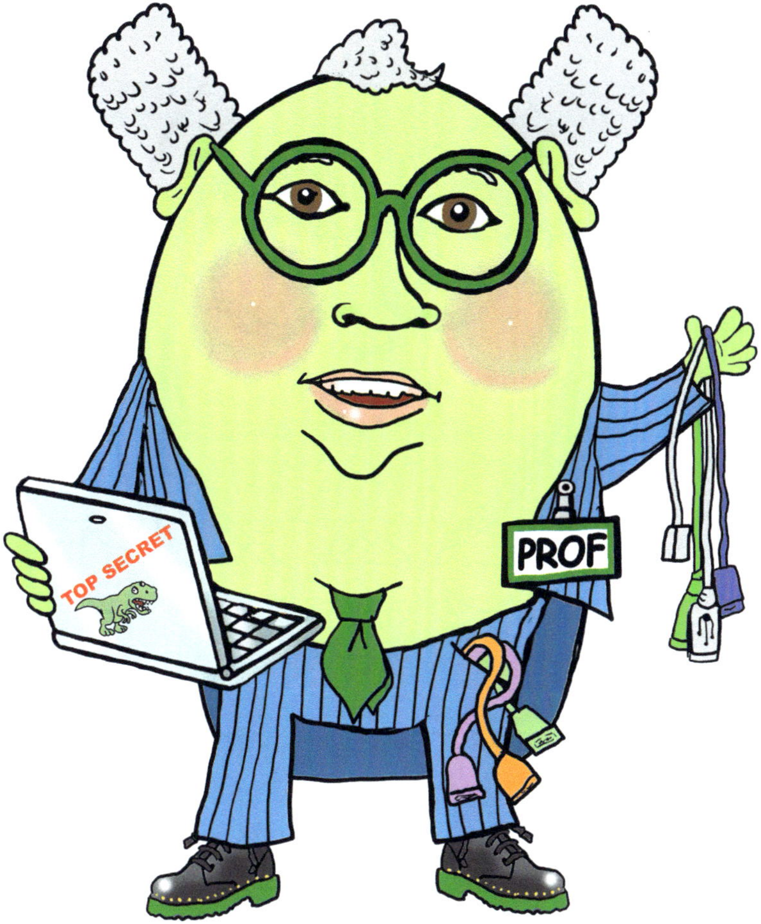
TOP SECRET
PROF

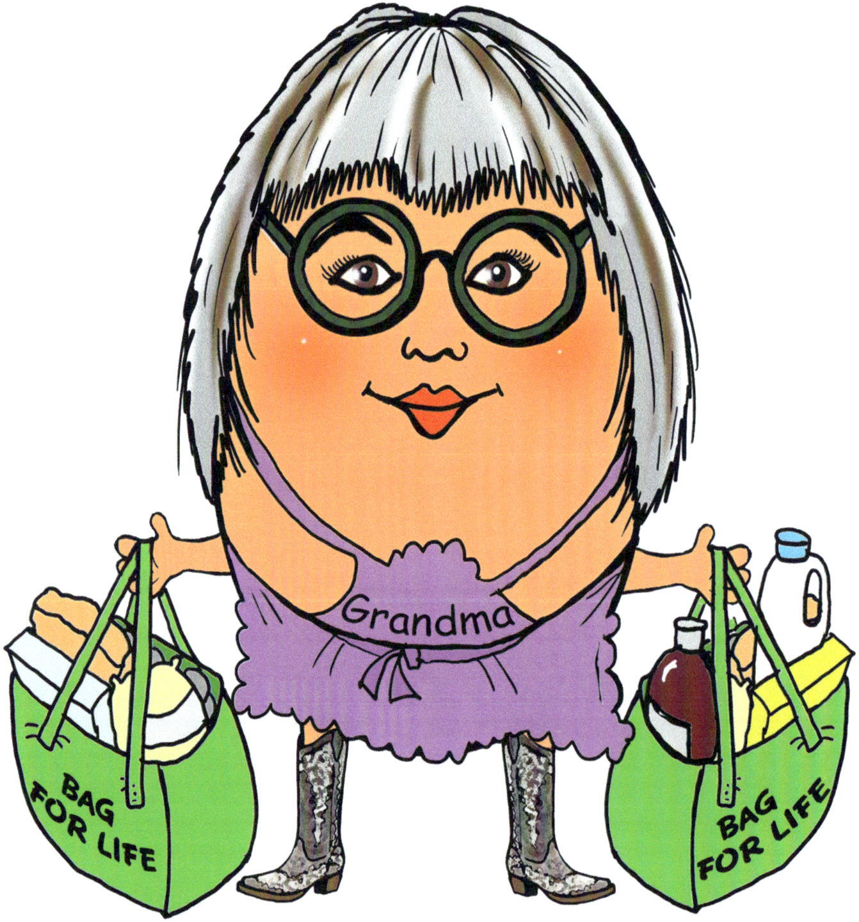
Grandma
BAG FOR LIFE
BAG FOR LIFE

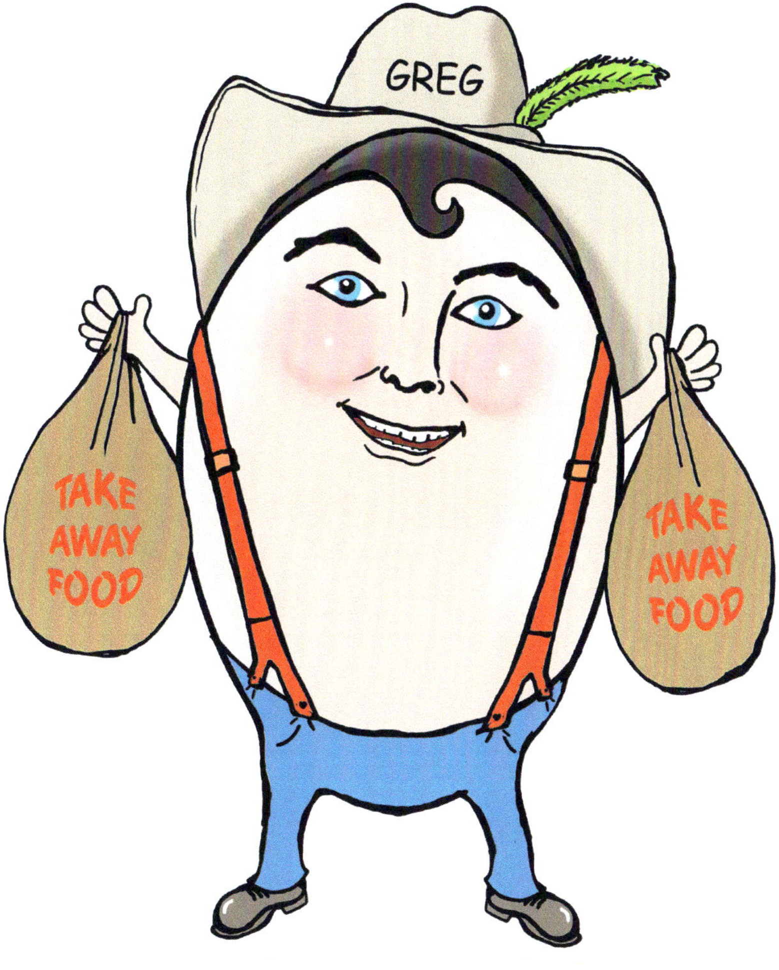
GREG
TAKE AWAY FOOD
TAKE AWAY FOOD

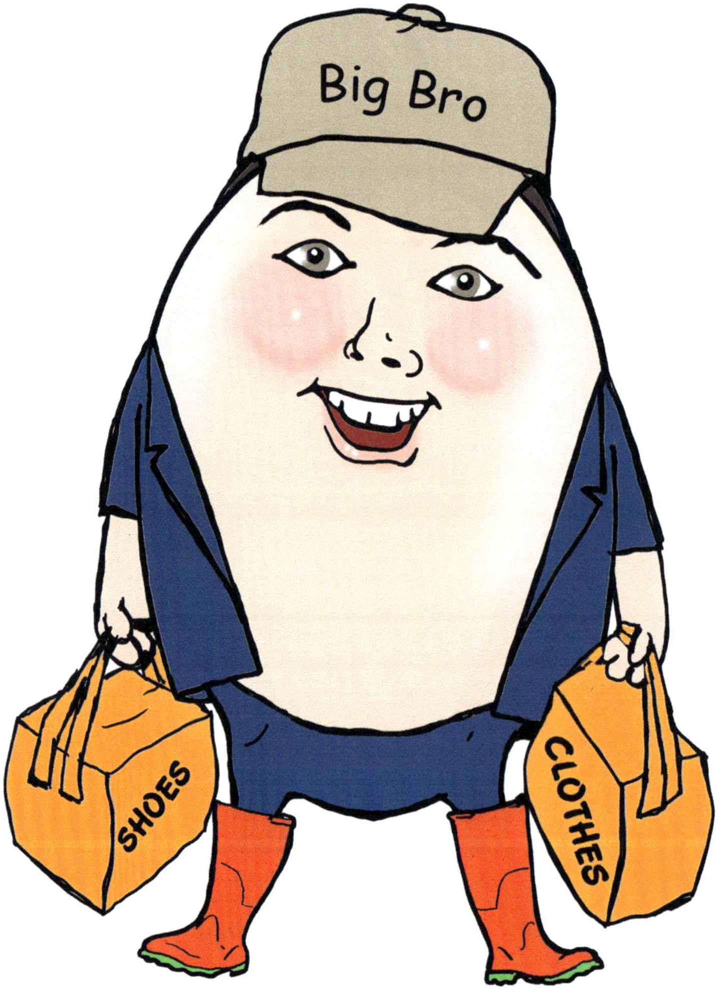
Big Bro
SHOES
CLOTHES

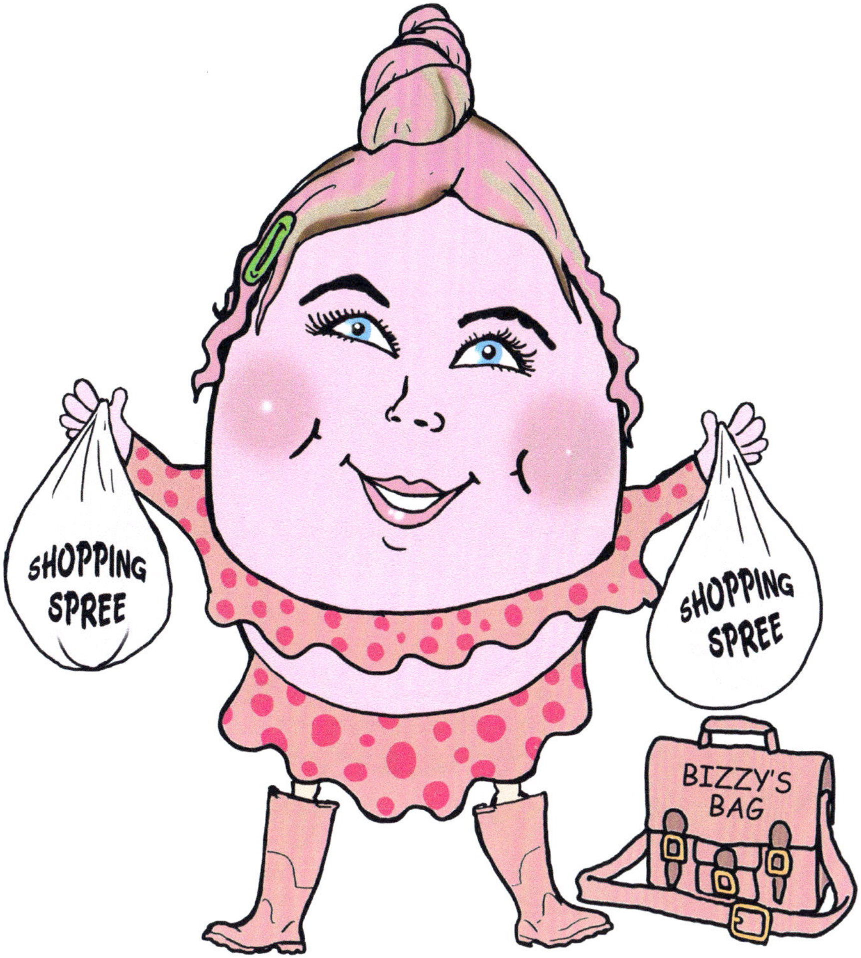
SHOPPING SPREE
SHOPPING SPREE
BIZZY'S BAG

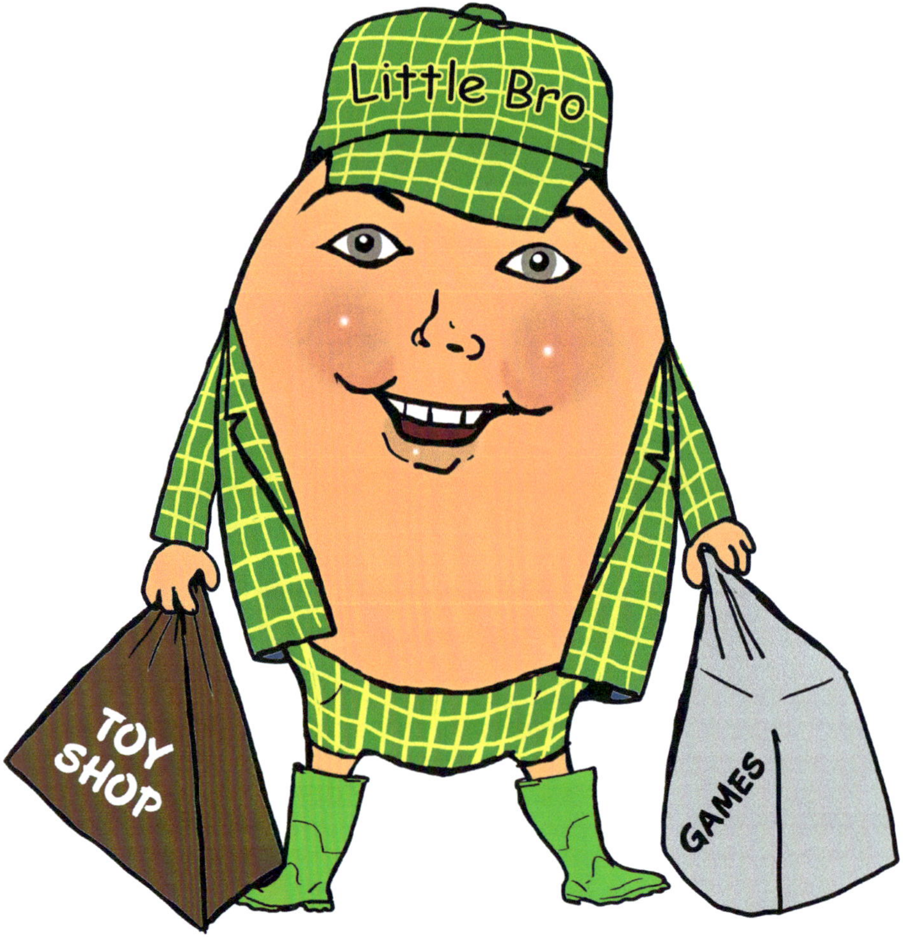
Little Bro
TOY SHOP
GAMES

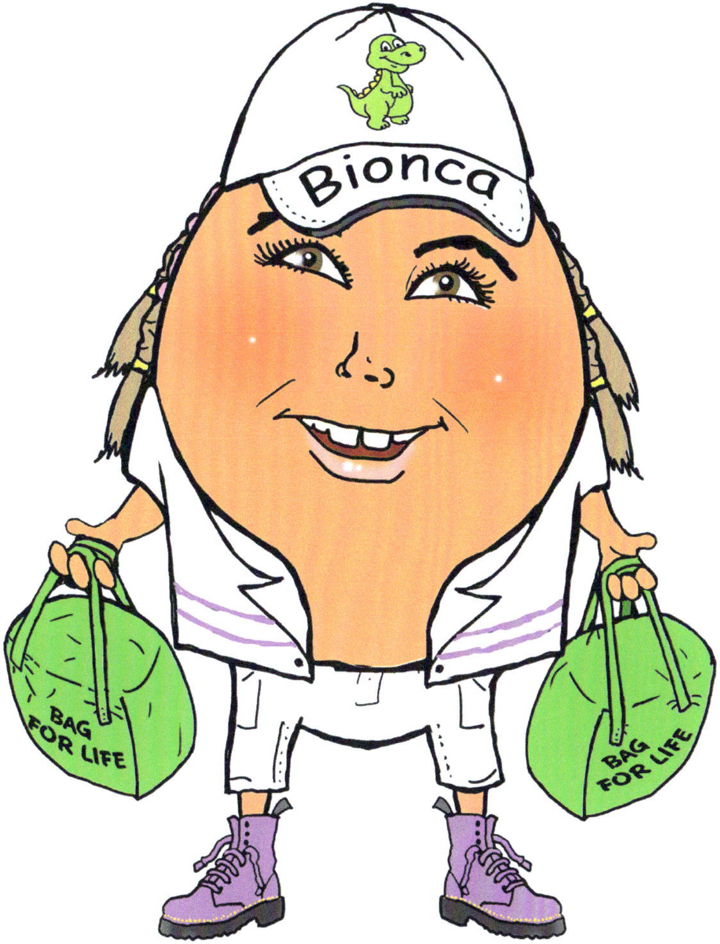
Bionca
BAG FOR LIFE
BAG FOR LIFE

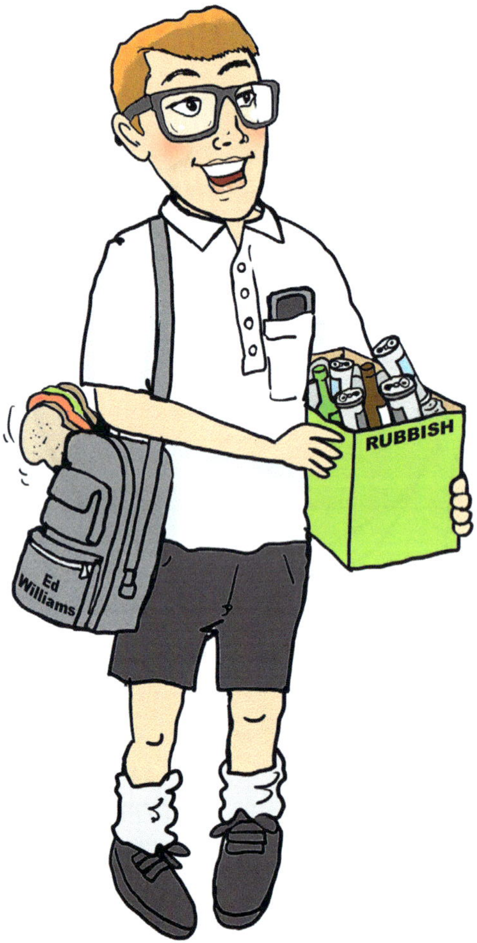
RUBBISH
Ed
Williams

SCOTTY
PLANET FRIENDLY
100 PERCENT BIODEGRADABLE
CLIMATE CHANGE
GLOBAL WARMING ALERT

LA-LA Forest Park

Well, isn't it winter?

Ferocious bouts of heatwaves hit LA-LA Forest Park grounds. The wintry season turns itself upside down into tinder-dry grounds. Once it boasted fresh natural countryside; now parched brittle bark fills the dehydrated parklands with crunchy curled-up rustic dead leaves blanketing the cracks in the pathways. The burst riverbanks blockade the muddy grounds which are now unfit for aquatic animals under siege by water pollution.

   The extra-dry drought is causing tree-damaging pests to thrive, spreading lava droplets, making millions of germs multiply its bacteria and viruses. The wildlife population are in total jeopardy and global warming is to blame. Relentless illnesses, homelessness and hunger now prevail over their innocent lives.

The blazing sun pulls in visitors to unwind in the idyllic ambience. Attractive 'posh sites,' burst at the seams close to the city dwellers, ending in triple-trouble for their natural inhabitants.

The mobile-camera, finger-clicking tourists rush to claim the home-from-home vacation hot-spot. The relief and relaxing touristy feeling get the visitors caught up in that photogenic perfect-picture postcard shot. Right now, nothing is going to stop them from relishing a well-earned retreat.

The grief-stricken deforestation allows more recreational activities. Endless outdoor leisure sports clog carbon footprints, the hiking and trekking woodland paths are worn away. The large groups bike the cycle trails, keen archery fanatics and golfers stomp through the rock-solid wildlife playground. The overexcited self-indulgent, endless inclusive first-class service get the holidayers blinded by nostalgia.

The suffering wildlife gags filth and fumes, the vacationers devour the frolicking popular energy-guzzling electronical cooling-down tubs simply called 'chilling-out.' The grounds lack respect from the tourists; it is treated as a human dumping magnetic field. The shop-until-you-drop spending-spree, 'I want it now,' madness continues.

LA-LA Forest Park's survival rate and life expectancy is under siege. Ignorance cannot see or hear the cries from the skies. Earth looks like a deep-plated pile of burnt toast.

The decision is made. The EggBangers handle the problem their way with a little help from the local wildlife inhabitants.

THE RECYCLOSAURUS AND EGGBANGERS

EggBanger Professor MicroChip has created two magnificent recyclable metal monsters. One is a gigantic recyclable hardworking megamachine called, The Recyclosaurus. The Springusaurus is the funday reward surprise who resides above the oasis, built from nothing less than unwanted recyclable rubbish.

The Recyclosaurus' 'Meeting Point' is where the overheated debates take place, usually about who is to blame for the mountainous smelly pollution.

The ramble hiking carbon footprints embed horse hoof marks. Plastic bottles and trekking print trails hide the routes to various footpaths. The human litterbugs are making litter-picking difficult for the ecowarriors.

The never-ending deforestation monster tree cutters create rising wildlife homelessness. The woodland animals are fleeing from their natural environment and into hazardous unnatural locations. Some live amongst the humans, in city districts, house gardens and village areas.

They home in underground sewers, tube stations, scavenging for food with their young ones.

The migration birds get lost in song, with the mass disappearance of migrating birds around the world. This is a warning sign that the planet is bamboozled by extreme climate change. Human activity is the likely cause of this problem.

The marine life and water plants that live in the salt waters in the oceans suffer the effects of mass ocean-fill pollution. The rough sea washes ashore mixes of plastic contamination on the beaches. The dry land and leaky streets are ambushed by bursting riverbanks. The lakes are affected by the chaotic aggressive rising sea levels.

The Antarctic shows signs of melting, causing high sea levels to flood. The mixture of clean river water and murky ocean floodwaters filter chemical poisonous substances. Tropical creatures tangle inside plastic and metal wiry particles. The ocean-pollution floating amongst the sea creatures tells a story that one day there could be more plastic in the ocean than fish.

Live festivals and great performances by musicians of all genres draw in thousands of fans to many resorts. People stomp carbon footprints, scanning for that perfect pitch where their beloved pets can run free.

The desirable characteristics of the fragrant wildflowers waft sweet aromatic smells that tempt visitors and tourist to free fresh-cut flowers while they last. LA-LA Forest Park offer the tourists plenty of memorabilia and dry wild-flower souvenirs.

The melodic sounds of wildlife reverberate a pleasurable stay in the countryside and woodlands. People congregate with picnic tables and portable gas-guzzling fire-rings for cooking. Campfire mouth-watering foods attract the hungry young wildlife. All the enticing fast-food appeals to the young while their parents find it difficult to hunt natural foods for them.

Large amounts of fancy colourful plastic and paper containers and packaging unseal the pleasant tasty takeaway meals: pizzas, hotdogs, kebabs and fish-and-chips, accompanied by flavoursome mouthwatering desserts and beverages. First class service for the posh lot brag the deli, crème-de-la-crème menus.

The idyllic posh sites — condos, log cabins, glamping and camping pitch domes, inflatable tents and caravan decoys — bait the sun-seeking getaway fanatics.

However, the sit-back-and-relax-by-fire-light, air-polluting barbecue-charcoal smoke and choking open-oven grills give the park a huge supply of carbon emissions. The non-electric vehicles — caravans, coaches, cars and motorbikes — exceed the levels of greenhouse gases. Nothing is off limits with plenty of free sunshine to go around. Wannabe golden-tan sunseekers spread the grounds with throw away dripping plastic bottles.

NO SCHOOL TODAY

The school kids shout. 'Hooray! Schools out for winter!'

Like clockwork, Crowlip curls her scrawny claws on the high wrought-iron school gate waiting eagerly for the kids to dash out. The old school is situated in the middle of the village. It is surrounded by large trees and grasslands with a long gravel path.

Crowlip scans her beady eyes for left-over sandwiches or wrap-scraps or the odd breadcrumb droppings from the loose-lid lunch boxes. Today, she thought it was going to be the usual long and tiring wait. The school bell rang earlier than the usual quarter-past-three in the afternoon.

She squawks, 'What! No way!'

Her claws don't feel frost bitten nor does she slip and slide backwards and forwards off the school gates. She's feeling something strange today.

She squawks. 'Steady on, kids!'

She gets herself in a kerfuffle. 'It's mid-morning, the children are overexcited and dashing in hoards down corridors. Why are they moving so fast clutching their school bags and mobile phones?'

She titters to herself. 'I'm a crazy bird. I'm dreaming. Isn't it supposed to be winter? Of course it's winter, stupid drip-snot crow. Then, why is my fluffy head sweaty and I feel hungry and thirsty?'

Autumn precedes what should be winter, which arrived only for a few days and leaves without notice. There's no sign of freezing chills nor a touch of frost, not even a droplet of rain or shuffling snowflakes wafting in the air, signals the first mark of, 'Extreme climate change.' It hits its highest peak, with arid scorching hot months and humid lazy days culminating in temperatures soaring up to forty degrees, or more.

The heat makes the children happy and hazy. Their school is now temporarily closed due to the weird heat wave. However, there's no escape from school homework. Everyone gets a school project to complete before the school reopens.

The school children scramble to the yellow school bus. They stomp over each other to claim their seats.

Ten-year-old, Ed Williams, attends the local village junior school. Ed wears large-rimmed reading glasses for long-sightedness. The weather forces him to wear summer school shorts and a short-sleeve white tee-shirt. Suddenly, Ed takes a hard tumble outside the school gates and lands flat on his face with the help from his nemesis – Nitty Nora the notorious school bully. She pushes Ed by launching a thuggish slap on his back. The flap on his school bag bursts open and scatters his stationery on the ground. He manages to pull himself up with both hands. His knees are covered with fresh grazes. He crawls on the hot gritty pathway towards the wide-open gate. The kids snicker and jeer loudly at him. They leap-frog over his back, Ed crouches until he thinks it's over. He quickly tries to grab his school stuff. He endures more slaps before he tumbles on the baked tarmac ground. Nitty Nora gets fed up with taunting Ed. She boards the school bus in fits of giggles.

    Ed is glad she is out of sight. He grabs his reading glasses and grapples with his mobile phone. He sits for a few seconds to regain his breath before ringing his grandad to let him know he'll be home early. He knows his grandad will be worried if he isn't home on time.

    Ed realises the phone screen is blurry but not quite smashed to smithereens. He manages to haul himself off the ground. He straightens up his clothes and dusts the muck off his shorts before firmly putting his specs back on. He gasps in complete horror. His mouth now wide open – the school bus has gone without him! The electronical school gates are slowly closing. Ed sees the school caretaker checking the digit-lock before scanning and checking that the school grounds are empty. Ed waits until the coast is clear which means he is free.

Ed smirks mischievously. He makes a sly decision not to ring his grandad. He daydreams what it would be like to have an adventure just for a day. He starts to whistle to his favourite song. He drags his feet kicking dry gravel stones. The sun-drenched heat makes his footsteps feel drudgery as he plods along. He clicks on unfinished mobile games not realising his phone is running out of battery life. Now he has gone right off the path. He doesn't realise a runaway dog and a fan-tailed black crow have been stalking him ever since he made his crafty move hiding behind the tree from the school caretaker.

He peers down at the whimpering staffy dog who has bolted from the dog catcher while Crowlip flutters behind. The menacing two get on Ed's nerves; he tries to dodge them at every opportunity.

Ed sees his school lunch flopping from his school bag flap. The dog and crow are scuffling over his ham-and-cheese-pickle sandwich.

Crowlip chatters. 'You four-legged flip-flop little dog turd! That sandwich is mine!'

Emee yaps. 'Let's not have any birdy tantrums. Woof! Woof!'

Emee continues. 'I'm starving and exhausted and in need of food. And, by the way I am not a little dog turd; I am a medium-sized, red-haired, brindle-tail, Staffordshire Bull Terrier. In fact, I'm so hungry I could swallow you up in one gulp! So, you go away, little drip snot turd!'

Crowlip snaps. 'No! I am not going anywhere. I was here first, it's my sandwich!'

Emee nips. 'Go and dig up a crusty wriggly worm to munch on with your bogey beak!'

Crowlip squawks. 'Right! I am going to snitch on you. The dog catcher will grab you good and proper and lock you up forever in the dog prison and throw away the key because you are a bad dog! Huh! Let's see how you like that!'

Emee barks. 'That's it! If you want war, I am going to give it to you!'

Crowlip resumes the name-calling. 'Hey there, doggy poopy doo, I bet you had to wear a muzzle on your sniffer nozzle, ha-ha-ha.'

Ed hears. 'Dog? You take the large piece. Crow? You can take the tiny bird-bite size.'

Crowlip grumbles. 'Satisfied, sloppy turd face?'

Emee fidgets. 'Mm. My waggling brindle tail is happy.'

The two got tired firing squawks and yaps at each other.

EMEE'S DOGNAPPED STORY

Crowlip chats. 'Huh! I'm pretty sure you haven't always been a runaway mutt. Tell me about your life-story, Lady Mutt?'

Emee yaps. 'When I was a puppy, I lived in a happy home. I slept in my own bed with a thick soft cuddly blanket and a pink and grey meerkat soft toy. It made me happy, ripping the stuffing out of it. I had lots of other toys to play with. I was more than happy ripping the stuffing out of them too. I had a purple-and-white dog collar with a sparkly matching lead. I remember the kind man and a little boy with red hair. We used to go for long walks and picnics. I wore a comfortable purple coat harness that rested over my back and buckled up under my belly. The kind man groomed me with my very own grooming set, which was after I had come back from the dog parlour. I didn't starve nor steal to feed myself, I always had good manners and pooped in a neat pile in the corner of the garden. It was easier for the pooper scooper to plop it into the scented bags before popping it in the dog-litter bin. I was trained to top-standard impeccable manners.'

Crowlip tweets. 'What a kind man to be putting up with you.'

Emee adds. 'Oh. I recall sniffing a powerful aroma around his pongy house slippers.'

Crowlip squawks. 'Pardon?'

Emee sighs. 'Mm. I miss resting my head on his stinky slippers.'

Crowlip yawns. 'Continue?'

Emee shudders. 'It began when I was playing in the garden on a sunny day, wriggling on the green lawn, wrestling with my skinny brindle tail running around in circles. Then, out of the blue, a trampy smelly bad man jumps over our garden fence and grabbed me. He stretched out his dirty long fingernails underneath my dog collar by the scruff of my neck until I dangled in the air, my back legs were wriggling with fright. Then he chucked me inside a stinky potato sack with tiny peep holes. I yapped so loud for the kind man to rescue me from the dog-napper, but he didn't hear me. No-one heard me. I think I heard an echo: "Pumpkin head, where are you!"

Crowlip scans. 'Mm. I must say that your head is a Halloweeny pumpkin shape.'

Emee chatters. 'I lived with that bad man for six long years. I slept on greasy newspaper fish-and-chips wrappers. All he did was shout and cuss, he forgot to feed me his scraps most of the time.'

Ed jolts. 'What!'

Emee yaps. 'We did have some good days. He took me out on the streets and tied a pink bow around my neck. When the bucket was full of cash, he was glad. I got hugs and photo shots and delicious dog treats from the people.'

Ed stomps. 'What a loser!'

Emee winces. 'As I got older and not so cute, no one gave us any money. He threw me out by the scruff of my neck. Then he decided to replace me with another puppy he got from somewhere. So, I hung around the tram-stops a lot. There were plenty of food scraps to choose from.'

Ed frowns. 'Sounds like he traded you in for a cuter puppy. He probably dog-napped that one from a forever home too.'

Emee whimpers. 'I hid everywhere. It was rough on the run to nowhere. I hid in garden bushes and was hungry all the time. I never stole from food bins on purpose. I got trapped in lots of rose bushes and prickly shrubs. It wasn't easy biting those prickly thorns out of my dog-butt. The dog catcher in the white prison van clutched his catch-pole to hunt me down. Somebody reported me as a stray. I gave the dog catcher a good chase because I can do high kangaroo jumps over fences. I scarpered like a racing whippet.'

Crowlip squawks. 'Tell me more?'

Emee staggers. 'I thought he stopped for a rest at one point and gave up on me. I peeped around every corner chuckling to myself because he had disappeared. I danced and pranced around with glee. He appeared from nowhere. He gripped my neck. I almost wriggled out of the catch-pole. He caught me good and proper this time. He gently put me back into the dog cage and gave me some treats. When we finally got to the dog-rescue prison, he unhooked the catch-pole from around my neck. It took a nanosecond for me to dart off again outside dog prison entrance. Does that answer your question, Crowlip?'

Crowlip blinks. 'Well, I suppose so. Actually, I feel speechless for tweets. If, you had gone with the dog catcher you would have got free food, a bed to sleep in, and rehomed.'

Emee remarks. 'Huh! I don't suppose you're still thinking about that ham-and-cheese-pickle sandwich. Like, having it all to yourself!'

Crowlip mutters. 'No! Emee, I feel sorry for you.'

Emee answers, 'I remember a little nuisance boy. It was just the three of us in our forever home. Who wants an eight-and-a-half-year-old stray dog?'

Crowlip implies. 'Mm. I suppose you are an old mutt now.'

Emee nips. 'Rude!'

Ed feels restless. He daydreams whilst fiddling with his phone trying to get a connection but unable to reach his grandad. He begins to like the idea of a new adventure. He thinks: 'If he took the LA-LA Forest Park route, his risk-taking quest might be worth it. He sees it as an excuse for research ideas for his school project.'

Ed sees happy people laughing in a hustle and bustle kind of way. He approaches them one by one for directions. They seem preoccupied with themselves. He starts to feel wobbly and lightheaded; from the carbon emission fumes, revving fuel engines and some non-electric motor vehicles playing loud music, spewing congestion through the entrance gates.

Emee chokes, while Crowlip decides to elevate flight above the grey smelly air.

Crowlip frowns. 'Hm. You won't believe what I just saw!'

Emee barks. 'What!'

Crowlip chatters. 'They're dumping rotten food and non-recyclable garbage! I reckon they should dump it in their own homes. Not ours!'

Emee yaps. 'Can you really see everything up there, Crowlip?'

Crowlip replies. 'No, but I've seen enough to report back to Professor MicroChip when I get to The Recyclosaurus' Meeting Point.'

Emee barks. 'Aaah, I know what you mean. A "saurus, like a dinosaur" the little nuisance boy had a huge green fluffy one that had a beastly monstrous grumble that sounded like, 'ROARRR! It made me, howl like a wolf.'

Crowlip squawks. 'I don't mean a toy dinosaur; it's more mechanically magnificent. Oopsy! I didn't say anything!'

Emee pants. 'Err. Yep. I heard you loud and clear. Spill the beans. I'm a dog, I know nothing. Anyway, I'm going to get myself a back-scratch against that brittle bark oak-tree stump over there, if you're not going to tell me anything. So, if you don't mind, just babble to your weirdo self.'

Crowlip mutters. 'No! Forget what I said, I'm just a stupid crow, with green hanging spaghetti-hoop snots.'

Emee moots. 'Okay, I see your beak is sealed and you're not going to spill the beans about the saurus.'

Crowlip ponders. 'Oh, dear. The Recyclosaurus is a lock-tight, super-top-secret recycle mega-machine hidden deep in the secret garden forest from the outside world. What am I going to do! I'm the biggest crow snitch in the whole world!'

The sun-baked drudgery walking makes Ed tired and very thirsty. He scans for the park ranger. They end up deeper into the hidden woodlands. The paths are caked up with leftover litter: slimy food slops, plastic gloves scattered everywhere. LA-LA Forest Park Ranger, Kane, is nowhere to be seen. Ed wonders if he's going to get home before dark. He is mindful that Emee needs to get to the Dog Rescue Centre.

Ed agitates. 'What's that scuffling and shuffling from behind those bushes?'

Crowlip tweets. 'I heard nothing?'

Emee yaps. 'It's a Yeti!'

Ed quivers. 'There's something shuffling in there alright.'

Crowlip squawks. 'It's an ugly sasquatch, let's go!'

Emee yaps. 'The bad man liked to watch the hairy Yeti big foot at telly time. They eat humans like Ed. They jump up high and climb trees and have a good swing about like a monkey.'

Crowlip squawks. 'Ed can't hear you. He only hears you yap.'

Emee replies. 'Okay. We hear each other and that's good enough for me.'

Crowlip answers. 'Sounds good to me too.'

Ed whispers. 'Let's hide behind the bushes.'

Emee woofs. 'Us two are safe — but he's not.'

Crowlip tweets. 'We could grab his bag and see if he's got some more food.'

Emee pants. 'Ed gave us his ham-and-cheese-pickle sandwich when we were squabbling over his leftover lunch. You can hover above that Yeti to safety, but we can't. Besides, there's no way you can fill that Bigfoot's hairy hungry belly! Look on the bright side: big-foot, Abominable Snowman, Yeti thingy will have a starter, main meal and a dessert, free of charge!'

Crowlip gets frantic. 'I can assure you, when I'm terrified; I taste like bird poop!'

Emee wriggles. 'Well, I've been scavenging from tram-stop dumpsters for years; I reckon I taste rank too.'

Crowlip wails. 'That would make us both the rankest snot-bag and poopy pooch snacks in the whole wide world. Mm. I think we are safe.'

Ed spots a rustic branch and swipes it along the bushes before poking around. That doesn't work because the Yeti doesn't come out. Emee begins to howl like a big bad wolf, but that doesn't work either. Crowlip threatens to hurtle a smelly turd on the Yeti's head.

Ed remembers. "Stranger danger! You're supposed to scarper! Scram! Come out you dirty punk!'

Crowlip chatters. 'What?'

Ed coaxes. 'I'll pretend to be that cool dude, Robin Hood, who used to hide in Sherwood Forest trees. I'll scoop out my bow and arrow and scare it away.'

Emee jumps. 'Just do it!'

Ed chants. 'Come out! Show your face and surrender!'

Crowlip chirps. 'Huh! Can't you tell Ed's on an adventure. He's one of those heroic outlaw archers. He'll attempt to steal from that Yeti, Bigfoot and fail miserably. We'll get fed to the wildlife because they're short of food right now.'

Emee puffs. 'That's not funny, you doofus crow!'

All three scuttle away taking sneaky peeps. They hear, 'Thud! Wallop!' A collision of pot-shot wild bushes forces the weird alien out of the prickly wild shrubs, trundling bumpety-bump carrying two plastic bags labelled: 'TOY SHOP' and 'GAMES.'

Little Bro hollers. 'Ouch! Stupid nettles have stung my little round buttcheeks! It's worse than an angry swarm of wasps. This is not happening!'

Ed yells. 'Kar-razee! Awesome!'

LITTLE BRO MEETS ED

Little Bro looks dapper in his green and yellow chequered patterned suit. He is wearing a smart matching jacket and shorts and wellington boots and a cap with his name on it that says, 'Little Bro.'

Little Bro cowers. 'I don't see you.'

Ed chortles. 'Mm. Yes, you can.'

Little Bro bleats. 'I can't hear you, and it's against The Woodlands Law for humans to look or speak to me. I'm a secret. Or maybe, I was a secret. Either way, I'm in triple-trouble now!'

Ed enquires. 'Woodlands Laws? Secret? What do you mean?'

Little Bro whinges. 'Don't speak to me. Don't leave a message because I won't get back to you.'

Crowlip tweets. 'Mm. I've always thought of you as the weirdo egg. What do you think Emee?'

Emee glares. 'He's a little bobbly egg, that's for sure.'

Ed remarks. 'Thank you egg boy, for talking to me. These two tag-along companions have done nothing but chirp, squawk, woof, yap and bark. I'm in trouble too. My school is closed because of the extreme weather changes. You know, it's supposed to be winter and it's sweltering humid hot. I got bullied by a girl and missed my school bus home. To top it all, I got lost again with these two quarrelling babbling buffoons at war to win my uneaten lunch. Apparently, the Park Ranger, is nowhere to be seen. My grandad will be worried if I'm not home on time. I'll be banned from my Xbox games and mobile phone. Even worse, not going to watch my favourite team, Nottingham Forest football match. I can't even get a YO connection. My phone battery is losing power. Help me! I, won't breathe a word. Besides, how could I explain I met an egg with a funny human face; eyes, arms and legs, carrying two bulky goody bags?'

Little Bro was familiar with YO signals, because Professor MicroChip has a helpful digital assistant and he never has problems with Wi-Fi connections. Little Bro knows that the Prof will be able to contact Ed's grandad. He begins to weigh up the pros and cons. He summarises: for a start no one will believe him, and Ed is just an adventure seeking silly sweaty school boy. Little Bro knows that Forest Park Ranger, Kane, has taken the last group of tourists on a trekking hike around the nature trails sight-seeing woodlands.

Crowlip squawks. 'Mm. Little Bro, have a good think what you're going to do with him.'

Little Bro conjures. 'He could do some rubbish collection, maybe the other EggBangers might accept him into the EggBangers clan for a day.' Little Bro knows Professor MicroChip and grandma EggBanger will make sure Ed gets home safely. Emee gets to the Dog Rescue Centre for rehoming.

Little Bro suggests. 'Ed how do you fancy helping us with our campaign rubbish collection? It's the only way to get you home.'

Ed cringes. 'Yuk! Okay. I'll collect those grunge bottles and fizzy pop cans. They'll fit in that green plastic box over there. Happy now? I know you think us humans are ruining this planet with our mass pollution but we're not all the same. My grandad and I are planet friendly. We know all living beings need clean air to survive. We recycle whatever we can: wheelie bins for rubbish, garden waste and recyclable litter in a separate dumpster. And, for your information, little egg-shell boy, I bet you didn't know that!'

Little Bro replies. 'Just look around you boy! Human litter critter!'

Ed rolls his eyes. 'Keep your hair on Bruv. Oopsy, you are bald.'

Little Bro squirms. 'Rude!'

Ed regrets. 'Please give me a chance. I've always heard great things about these touristy sites. And I promise you, I will collect as much as I can. Argh!'

Little Bro glares. 'I need you to swear that you will never, ever, breathe a word to anyone outside LA-LA Forest Park.'

Ed promises. 'I swear. I'll lock that secret in my brain even if it gives me a bubbling headache.'

Little Bro instructs: 'Do three hi-fives, followed by a salute and spit. Then repeat: "No nudges, no grudges."

Little Bro asks. 'What's your favourite food?'

Ed answers. 'I love baked beans followed by a bowl of hot chocolate pudding. It's the best food ever, only on a school day.'

Little Bro ponders. 'Playing a horrible trick on a lost boy would be one of the worst guilty offences ever. There would be a promise of triple chores and no fundays or treats for a very long time. It excites him with the thought of, 'harmless-naughtiness' and it wouldn't count as being bad.' Therefore, he wouldn't get into any bother with the Prof.

Little Bro whispers. 'I'm serious.'

Ed shrieks. 'Ugh! Kar-razee gross! That's seriously disgusting, Bruv!'

Little Bro resumes. 'Now Bruv, you must say this, three times without blinking or gagging your guts up. And, you're not allowed a sick-bag.'

Ed replies in a gruff voice. 'Do I have to?'

Little Bro waves his pointy finger. 'Say this yukky poem now!'

Ed agrees; 'Okay! Okay! I'll do it Bruv!'

"I swear on Little Bro's oath,
I will keep my big gob shut,
If, I, Ed Williams, do snitch I will get stitches in my trouser britches,
Full of creepy crawly biting mites, causing me a big fright,
My chocolate pudding bowl, will now be a baby's potty crown,
My baked beans will turn into squidgy bugs and slugs,
I, must gobble the lot until my plate is pristine clean,
I will not frown nor make a sissy sound."

A R Trent

Ed completes. 'Get me an extra-large sick-bag. Now!'

Crowlip pukes. 'Shall we get him a plastic boffing bag?'

Emee gags. 'I'll go fetch that plastic bag whiffling through the branches.'

Ed gains Little Bro's trust. In no time, they all set off collecting pongy rubbish. Either way he knows he's in big trouble.

Crowlip titters. 'I am sick of poop picking for them bow-wow-pooch butts, everywhere I hop there's a smelly refill mutt bag! You can't mix and match poop bags with these little electronic gadgets. Why do I get these hopping-ugh! Chores?'

Emee yaps. 'Don't look at me or else I will snap off one of your snotty green pimples from that cranky beak with my razor-sharp nippy teeth!'

Little Bro interjects. 'Listen up! You two can bark and squawk all you like. This is all down to the scruffy tourists! They bring their pets who run around thinking they own the place!'

Ed enquires. 'What do you mean?'

Little Bro convulses. 'Firstly, those dogs go rampaging all over, playing catch ball with their beloved owners. Get the picture? All, la-de-dah-de-dah, I love my mutt! Then, those pooches decide to stop for poop machine-breaks in between. And, let's face it, where do some of them dogs put it all, because their butt-cheeks aren't that big!? Secondly, the dog owners scoop the first rapid missile link. And thirdly, those warm filled bulging bags are dumped anywhere on the hot grounds. The smearing aroma is so gagging – and the tourists are too lazy to use the dog-waste dumpsters provided everywhere!'

Crowlip comments: 'I do think you've overlooked the size of some of those butt-cheeks!'

Emee pants. 'I can vouch for that. Dog butt-cheeks come in small, medium, large and extra-large shapes and sizes.'

Ed screeches. 'Eeeeek!! No more talking about sloppy-plops or smelly-poop splats, please!'

Emee cups her jaw. 'Before you ask, I scoop my own poops. Look! My very own poop bag! What dog does that? Woof! Woof! Oh. Yes. You can believe it. I was trained to no less than one-hundred-percent, well-bred behaviour from the kind man.'

Little Bro concludes. 'Now the dog-plop saga is out of the way, let's carry on with our chores. And by the way. Crowlip? If you're flying to the Posh sites soon, make it a fleeting flight, and don't you or them gulls eat all the free junk food scraps. We'll meet you at The Recyclosaurus Meeting Point later.'

Emee yaps. 'I hope there's plenty of dog kibble. I'm starving.'

Crowlip squawks. 'It's difficult to dodge those nature trails; criss-cross biking and hiking trails, or bird-watching hide fanatics at the nearby fishing lakes.'

Little Bro warns. 'Crowlip? You know the rules. Blute won't be very happy with you unless you come up with a convincing cover-up story as to why you haven't turned up with any recyclable trash. We all know your taste buds can sniff fodder from afar. Especially around the log cabins, condos, yurts and glamping sites.'

Crowlip twists her beak. 'How dare you suggest such a thing!'

Ed interjects. 'The temptation may be too much for you because you are a greedy crow!'

BIZZY AND BIONCA

EggBangers, Bizzy and Bionca, are busy collecting recyclable paper: catalogues, newspapers, books and magazines and designer shopping bags. The nearby stables and equestrian houses host champion racehorses and potential prize-winning colts. There's plenty of torn-up betting slips scattered around the sites. Even the odd pigeon carrier makes the odd betting slip blunder around the wind turbines.

Bizzy's favourite colour is pastel pink. She wears clothes with matching pink wellington boots. Her pink satchel has long straps with her name tag. She is good at spotting unwanted shopping-spree bags. Bizzy is very glamourous. She wears her hair up in a bunch with ringlets that sway from side-to-side, pinned back and adorned with a green clip.

Bionca adores the colours purple and white. Her cap is white with the 'Recyclosaurus' logo' imprint. She wears a matching suit with purple laced-up boots. Her hair is well-groomed with braids. Her hair flicks backwards and forwards, styled to match her perfect complexion.

Bionca is an adventurous EggBanger, she likes climbing trees and is always on the look-out for potential fly-tippers. She tucks her binoculars inside her jacket pocket and often clambers up trees to retrieve plastic bags from branches while scanning for fly-tippers. The equestrian sites are danger zones. A bluster of wind can blow a plastic bag over the head and eyes of a horse. This makes the horses bolt. Riding lesson hours can be busy for her as she mounts up trees bending and stretching.

    Bionca clambers. 'Look! Those two men just dumped a shabby stained rusty springy mattress and a mini-fridge freezer.'

    Bizzy ushers. 'Have a fumble for your binoculars to get a clear view of the crime.'

    Bionca whispers. 'I'll zoom in. Gosh! A stolen rusty supermarket shopping-trolley with car tyres squashed in, whizzing down a dry grassy bank. Crikey! Now they're struggling with the weight by pushing and kicking and cursing at the old cranky trolley.'

Bizzy gasps. 'Wait for it. There's a large plastic tub wobbling on top of a cart filled with unimaginable dirty rags and tattered shoes.'

Bionca replies. 'Yep! Those litter-critter, fly-tipping humans are at large again! Take a look, Bizzy.'

Bizzy responds. 'No thanks, my outfit isn't tailored for such torture!'

Bionca blinks. 'Oopsy.'

Bizzy gags. 'Bionca, not again! You've let a cracking gust of fossil fuel flatulence out of your white combat trousers.'

Bionca shushes. 'Blame it on those fuel cooking gadgets for my uninvited big rip!'

Bizzy questions. 'Did you see anything else up there?'

Bionca fumes. 'Yes, I did. A monstrous sack of rubble rocks thrusting into a lilypond. And another tatty mattress. Oh! No! That lilypond is now a filthy whirlpool dumpster!'

Bizzy shrills. 'Gosh! The water homes are in ruins and unfit to home the aquatic creatures. Ducky and Froglips will be furious.'

Bionca urges. 'Be quiet Bizzy.'

Bizzy whispers. 'Why?'

Bionca says. 'I think I hear a whimpering sound. I'll go and investigate who or what is making that troublesome blubbing sound.'

Bizzy warns. 'Be cautious of that footling redhaired fox, Nasty Patsy trickster!'

Bionca replies. 'Huh! She doesn't scare me!'

Bizzy implores. 'Patsy doesn't whimper; she roars like a fierce lioness. She thinks she's the queen of the forest park jungle. Everyone knows she's LA-LA Forest Park's biggest gangster game-player! And that bully is no Queenie!'

Bizzy retorts. 'Bionca? We must find out. Ugh! Please fan off your noxious fossil fuel fart first. Patsy will sniff you out with that nauseous pong. Let's edge forward to the cries.'

Bionca hollers. 'Nay! It's you! Are you hurt? Where's your big brother Robby! Aww. You are stuck in a filthy plastic bag. It's full of large sharp nails, metal wires, knives and forks left by the happy campers. You poor thing!'

Nay shivers. 'I was bobbing up and down, jigging along looking for Robby. I wanted the tourists to see me clutching my banner. I accidentally took a shindig hop into a reeking plastic bag. Both my legs are tangled inside this metal trap. It smells worse than rotten eggs. I'm sorry for using the egg word.'

Bizzy chortles. 'Well. On this poor occasion let's untangle you first. Robby will be getting on with his cleaning duties. He'll catch you up at The Recyclosaurus' Meeting Point later. You can tell everyone what happened to you today.'

SCOTTY AND BIG BRO

Meanwhile, EggBanger Greg, Scotty and Big Bro actively blitz the camp sites. It's a never-ending collective task. The day-trippers never fail to leave half-eaten slimy yoghurt pots and greasy sloppy margarine tubs around. Greg concentrates on the junk-food takeaway plastic containers and the contaminated soft paper packaging – food boxes purchased from kebab, pizza, hotdog and cheeseburger on-site eateries. Take-away bag assignments are a smutty chore, the grimy junk food cartons, plastic straws and cutlery are often seen racing down the streams. The heat-related cluster of crowd-pulling mosquitos flock to the debris.

Greg wears a stylish Stetson hat with an adorn green feather spearing tucked at the side. His long tight blue trousers have red braces. He wears brown lace-up shoes.

EggBanger Scotty wears a smart blue tartan print with matching footwear. His work is tiresome. The thick fabric and extreme heat make it difficult for him to work. He carries heavy collections such as ice-cooler bags and hot food in metal and plastic containers.

Greg and Scotty spot Robby trundling the pebble hiking path jibber-jabbering to himself.

Robby shouts. 'I can't find my little sister, Nay. Has anyone seen her?'

Scotty bellows. 'Nae, Robby, we haven't seen the bonnie wee lassie today.'

Robby stutters. 'I must find her before Nasty Patsy claps eyes on her. Nay hopped off to find a toy to play with and wanted to make her own banner for the tourists to see. That was two-hours ago.'

Greg concurs. 'I'm sure Nay will be waiting for you at The Recyclosaurus.'

Robby blurts. 'I think I should go and look for her. You know I'm the only rabbit at LA-LA Forest Park, who can't hop!'

Greg and Scotty cackle. 'Yes, we know you can't hop, but you can bolt off faster than a cheetah.'

Robby warns. 'Let's not forget, if Patsy catches Nay, the worst will happen. It would only take one mouthful to gobble her up. Besides, I would miss having my little sister around.'

Greg suggests. 'You tag along with us. The more paths we trek, one of them might lead us to Nay's pawprints.'

Robby blurts. 'If it's okay with you, I think I will bob off and search for Nay myself.'

Scotty prompts. 'Take heed, gangster Patsy will gobble you up as well.'

Robby remarks. 'I'll make sure I super sniff her out with my twitchy nose and use my rabbit radar ears and antenna whiskers. I hope Nay reaches The Recyclosaurus meeting point safe and sound.'

Big Bro arrives. He wears blue shorts and a matching jacket, red wellington boots and a light brown cap with his name on it.

Big Bro greets. 'Hi guys. I've got a good idea, do you want to hear it?'

Scotty retorts. 'If it's anything to do with getting our chores done quicker, then I'm in.'

Big Bro agrees. 'I was just going to say that.'

Greg adds. 'Ugh! I kid you not, these takeaway bags smell like splodges of chunky hot slops.'

Big Bro gags. 'Argh!'

Chéree the red squirrel whooshes. 'Ouch! Get this spikey fork off me!'

Scotty remarks. 'Bonnie wee lassie, I'll get you out.'

Chéree quivers. 'Thank goodness! It's you.'

Greg asserts. 'What happened?'

Chéree sobs. 'The grey squirrels have been chasing me for hours. It's been like an obstacle course, jumping over camping equipment. Total write-offs they are! Those horrid grey squirrels wanted to steal my red cherry. The visitors threw it at me to shoo me away but it clonked me on the head instead. I was only being a good ecowarrior collecting nuts and bolts to take to The Recyclosaurus.'

Scotty replies. 'Nae. The grey squirrels don't like you red squirrels.'

Chéree enquires. 'But, why? What have us red squirrels done to them? We're virtually extinct! Anyway, one cherry wouldn't be enough for those greedy grey gits!'

Scotty answers. 'Chéree, the truth is, red squirrels have lived in England for thousands of years. Once upon a time. The grey squirrels were the visitors.'

Chéree adds. 'Do you mean like the tourists that overstay their welcome?'

Scotty answers. 'Aye, I suppose so. Let's not forget they've lived here for a very long time. They wouldn't find their way back to their original habitats.'

Chéree replies. 'I still don't understand what you're saying.'

Scotty adds. 'Well. The grey squirrels were brought here, some escaped and multiplied in parks and gardens. I heard, they can be very mischievous, biting outdoor buildings and household wires. They became established as a wild population towards the late eighteen-hundreds. The worse part for your population, Chéree, is that the grey squirrels carried their own diseases with them. I regret to say that masses of red squirrels died because they couldn't survive the grey squirrel viruses.'

Chéree demands. 'Tell me more!'

Scotty continues. 'Most of your family and friends and other red squirrels from the past were living in wild locations in Scotland and North England protected by law set by the humans.'

Chérée stutters. 'I don't want to catch the grey-squirrel pox.'

Scotty replies. 'Nae. Don't you worry Chérée. Aye. You're safe on our watch.'

Bizzy and Bionca emerge with little Nay. 'Hi there?'

Greg blinks. 'I see you've found Nay. Robby is looking for her, he bolted off like a cheetah in a big hurry.'

Bizzy and Bionca inform. 'Fly-tippers have mastered the art of fly-tipping. They're stealing trolleys from supermarkets and rearranging them into pushing dumpster carts. Let's not forget about the messy tourists rubbishing our grounds as well.'

Greg declares. 'This is war! I have an idea that'll teach those pesky tourists a lesson. I can't do much about the fly-tippers today. The Plan A is a trial bag. Drastic action means; move forward with the Plan B bags. If Plan A fails, Plan B, won't!'

Bizzy and Bionca interjects. 'Mm. Tell us more?'

Greg explains. 'I designed a universal tourist bag with Professor MicroChip's help a while back. I hadn't put the idea into practice until now. It's free of charge for the visitors. I'm putting bags in each accommodation on every site – with a little help from our wildlife ecowarrior comrades.'

Nay cries. 'No more nasty plastic bags!'

Bizzy explains. 'Nay was trapped inside a polluted bag full of sharp objects that stuck in her little body.'

Greg explodes. 'That's why these large bags are brilliant. They're not plastic, or metal nor harmful to anyone or the environment. They're made from tough seaweed grass. Look! They're one-hundred-percent chemical free, and nearly seventy-percent carbon emissions free. Huh! The humans ought to do themselves a favour and take one. It's definitely compostable and planet-Earth friendly. Professor MicroChip and I feel this is a way forward.'

Scotty urges. 'Show us the bag.'

Greg grins. 'The Plan A bag or Plan B bag?'

A PLANET FRIENDLY BAG
TOUGH SEAWEED GRASS
CHEMICAL FREE
COMPOSTABLE SOIL
UP TO 75% CO^2 EMISSIONS FREE

Big Bro interjects. 'Argh! Plan A bag won't work. Greg Bruv, I'd go straight to the Plan B bag.'

Greg replies. 'I think you're right. I'll pass it by Professor MicroChip straightaway.'

Scotty interjects. 'Hahaha. Watch your back tourists; we've got the Plan B bags!'

Greg laughs. 'Yep! I'll round up the ecowarrior birds with nimble claws because they can drop those Plan B bags discretely in every accommodation on every site.'

Bionca affirms. 'Yes, go straight to Plan B. If you saw what Bizzy and I witnessed today, you would scrap the Plan A bag in a flash!'

Bionca bickers. 'You can't put a mattress in a bag.'

Bizzy titters. 'I was just saying, don't take me literally.'

Greg contemplates. 'Mm. I think you have a point.'

Bionca states. 'Those tourists shop until they drop into a semi-comatose shopping state. Their spending sprees get out of hand, dumping their unwanted clothes for the next-best-thing. I-want-it-now factor, look at me. Ooh, la-la, I'm the 'it' factor. I'm so adorable! As a matter of fact, I'm too adorable for myself. Just ask Bizzy.'

Bizzy retorts. 'Rude!'

Bionca laughs. 'I'm just saying. You wear hand-me-down recyclable exquisite clothes and accessories. Your merch matches your beautiful EggBanger, you. Oh, and you have a delightful pink satchel.'

Bizzy rolls her eyelids. 'What do you mean?'
Bionca grins. 'Bizzy, the one and only EggBanger fashion icon?'

GREG'S PLAN-B BAG

The EggBangers chat about the purpose of the Plan B Bag.

Bionca interjects. 'Erm. What makes you think the tourists will take any real notice of the Plan B Bags, Greg?'

Greg rubs his chin. 'Well, let me see. It's a bit like confiscating their precious goodies then taking them to LA-LA Forest Park's lost-property.'

Big Bro smirks. 'I know the lost property is miles away which will anger them. But, how can stealing from the tourists help them?'

Greg continues. 'Plan B is snaring and daring. I admit it's a risky business. But some of those litter louts just won't stick to the recycling rules! Plan B aims to infuriate them good and proper.' 'It's not rocket science.'

Bizzy sighs. 'Sounds like the best chores ever!'

Scotty adds. 'Aye, how difficult is it for them to remember, reduce and reuse and recycle in that order? Then again, nae bother themselves.'

Greg interjects. 'I'm sick of picking up half-filled soggy cartons off the grounds. I see electronic gadgets with goo stuffed inside them. And, it doesn't half reek like Scotty's cheesy socks.'

Scotty replies. 'Aye Greg. Thanks for that comment, big man.'

Greg points out. 'Some tourists don't bother themselves with recycling bins.'

Scotty grins. 'Aye. But why bring my cheesy socks into the equation?'

Nay adds. 'They're scruffy, sloppy and messy, and I don't like them. I think we should put teeny weeny baby slugs on their lovely fluffy pillows at nighttime when they're fast asleep. That will give them a big shock, just like the one I got!'

Bizzy laughs. 'Nay, we're just trying to teach them a basic lesson.'

Little Nay puckers. 'They're bad, and I don't like them because I saw two beautiful, frightened butterflies in distress: a Zebra swallow tail and a Red Admiral butterfly stuck in a hot smelly yoghurt pot instead of a buddleia sweet-smelling shrub. And I think those tourists are just going to ditch those Plan-B bags whether you like it or not!'

Bionca points out. 'Quick! Go and pass this by Professor MicroChip because stealing is still wrong no matter how much you flower it up.'

Greg replies. 'Hm. I think you're right. The Prof is chief gaffer around these parts.'

Greg decides. 'Hey guys! I'm going to scoot off to the other sites to see if I can round up some less busy eco-bird-warriors on my way to Professor MicroChip's work-shed in the Secret Garden. I hope their nippy claws are pristine clean for the job.'

Scotty replies. 'Aye Greg, we can't have cloggy claws on the bag mission.'

Big Bro states. 'If you happen to see Little Bro, can you remind him to meet me at The Recyclosaurus? I haven't seen him since he wandered off earlier today. Knowing him, he's being a nuisance somewhere, sneaking up on someone around LA-LA Forest grounds.'

Greg shouts. 'Hey, you two birds! What are you doing around these parts?'

Piérre tweets. 'I shouldn't be here, I'm lost. It's extremely hot for this time of the year. Since leaving France my head feels all giddy, I found it difficult to follow the migrating song.'

Anushka interjects. 'I'm from India and I'm lost too. My flock were singing together and then I lost my way and forgot the song.'

Greg replies. 'Oh, dear. I think you'd better follow me. I see you have clean nippy claws that can assist me with my Plan B bag mission. I'll explain on the way.'

Anushka squawks. 'We came across two migration birds, one was a dodgy bird called Citrus, the other is his companion, Magenta. They are

Caribbean migration birds. Citrus suggested we tagged along with them. But, we said no.'

Piérre chatters. 'That old shifty bird, Citrus, had racing pigeons on his mind. I said, no, no, no. I'm not going near those wind turbines!'

Greg affirms. 'You did the right thing, Piérre.'

Piérre and Anushka decide. 'We can be ecowarriors for a day.'

Greg hears squealing. 'You look like a couple of farm animal escapees, huffing and puffing like a steam train engine. I see you having difficulty walking?'

Anushka eavesdrops. 'They seem to be stumbling and hobbling.'

Digby squeals. 'Ouch! My poor shins!'

Greg shouts. 'You're pigs!'

Jax crouches. 'Yes. We are pigs in a dilemma. Err. Hello, I'm Jax and this is my friend Digby. He's cut his trotters by tripping over a tree stump. Not sure, could have been some broken metal bits. My trotters aren't having a good time either. The area is full of half-dismantled, abandoned camping equipment. Total write-offs, I might add.'

Digby interjects. 'It's been a one-after-another disastrous journey having to scarper through a rip-roaring circus pirate entertainment show.

Through acrobatic flips and fire stunts, knights on horseback swinging swords in the air on sandy gritty grounds. The castle theme was dark and full of spooks and ghouls which was quite an ordeal for us. Might I mention, these areas are very much in need of a thorough clean-up.'

Greg replies. 'It's funny you should mention that, because I'm looking for more helpers to collect recyclable and non-recyclable rubbish left by the tourists.'

Digby chortles. 'Look at me – I'm wounded! I feel like a soldier at war. And, I'm covered in hot-pot mushy peas including unidentified grimy slops!'

Greg replies. 'Welcome to the EggBangers world. I understand your dilemma. I've had the honour of scraping up those slops.'

Jax replies. 'We know. We can smell you.'

Greg enquires. 'What's your story, pigs? How did you get here? These parts are normally for the wildlife and let's not forget the paying tourists.'

Jax interjects. 'Well, it goes like this – we do not want to be food! And, certainly not served on a platter at Suzy's thirteenth birthday party bash. Get the picture Greg? The kid's sausage surprise menu.'

Greg replies. 'You two don't seem to have much luck today, do you?'

Jax adds. 'We were chosen from the other pigs on the farm. Farmer Giles thought we were the most succulent-looking chunky pigs! Can you believe it? Just us two, delicious enough for food at Suzy 's birthday party tomorrow! And we thought we were his precious, prize-winning, treasured pigs!'

Greg ponders. 'Mm. You've cut your trotters sure enough so I suppose there's not much you can help me with today.'

Jax interjects. 'I can work. Please don't leave us because we've nowhere else to go. We darted from the farm before because we didn't want to be Christmas dinner!'

Digby whispers. 'Shush. Don't mention the Scotch-egg word. And, yes. I know, Greg looks like an egg.'

Jax hushes. 'We should be grateful we've found ourselves a real bodyguard. Shut up and listen to what he's got to say. Our lives depend on this new mate.'

Digby agrees. 'I'm sorry for mentioning the 'egg' word but I was just wondering that's all.'

Jax warns. 'Don't, mention the Scotch-egg word again or else we will have a special invite to Suzy's birthday party tomorrow!'

Greg backtracks. 'Why did you run away?'

Jax sobs. 'It was just a few days before Christmas, might I add, it was quite chilly on the farm. Farmer Giles stomps into the pigsty having a right old chuckle to himself. He was rubbing his hands and kicking his muddy boots in the air, doing his Billy-no-mates tap-dance. He didn't take into consideration that we eat pigswill so how can we be appetizing?'

Greg listens with undivided attention. 'So, what happened after farmer Giles spotted you two prize-winning pigs as the prime suspects for the Christmas dinner nosh?'

Jax hollers. 'My piggy brain is having a tizzy moment. I can't squeal, snort or give an oink right now.'

Digby squeaks. 'Oh, my piggy-wiggy trotters, we were in line for "pigs in blankets."'

Greg gasps. 'Oh. My Gosh! Is there anything else to add?'

Jax snorts. 'Oven-baked, sausage rolls, ham and cheese vol-au-vent stuffing, bacon strips top-notch trimmings on the three-birds' lavish centrepiece silver platter. Then plonked on Granny's rotating lazy-Susan spinning table-top, surrounded by Yorkshire pudding and stuffing balls for the Christmas dinner feast. Blaaaaah!'

Jax oinks. 'Oh. Yes. Quite chilly we were on the run. Huh! Maybe in need of a warm fluffy duvet. But, "pigs in blankets" posing in a slab position on Granny's best platter would not have been a pretty sight!'

Greg flabbergasts. 'You're safe now. Maybe, you could join us with our clean-up campaign. Any little help makes teamwork.'

Digby snuffles. 'Okay. But it will be a struggle.'

Jax huffs and puffs. 'Mm. Okay. I'll try, but it will be difficult.'

Greg glances. 'Hey! Hedgehogs! What's up?'

Skipper and Scamp weep. 'We've been plodding along dodging lumps and bumps.'

Greg remarks. 'Not again! You two are supposed to keep close to the riverbanks, aren't you?'

Scamp explains. 'The muddy riverbanks are flooding because the Antarctic glaciers are melting. The movement of water in the oceans, streams, rivers and ponds are giving us a hard time right now.'

Greg affirms. 'Nothing new there.'

Skipper says. 'The rivers are swamped with water garbage. Our coats are flexible and soft, but we have thick layers of spikes because our keratin quills are matted up in gunge. The plastic rainbow particles smother our coats. It's difficult and dangerous for us because we already have difficulty seeing. There are trillions of tiny plastic pieces in the water. They've floated from the ocean into our rivers and on our riverbanks.'

Scamp whimpers. 'The currents swept us up, we only went for a loop-de-loop splash in the shallow streams.'

Skipper wept. 'Our eyes are stinging from oil-slick plastics. The overspill covered us. Our eye-sight isn't the best as you know. We sniffed our way through stale foods. That's when we spotted Nay. She was sobbing. We grabbed as many knives, forks and spoons from her plastic bag prison.'

Greg retorts. 'Why take the dangerous route on the busy roads?'

Scamp answers. 'We fancied a puddle dive, splish-splash from the burst riverbanks to get a refreshing shower on this very hot and humid day.'

Scott interjects. 'What has brought you two to these parts amongst the human carbon footprints. It must be like digging yourselves out of the trenches.'

Skipper answers. 'We got stuck at the crossroads on the zebra-crossings. We ended up at LA-LA Forest Park's entrance. The traffic slowed down for the smug-looking tourists, but not for us! They were almost on top of us. The thunderous roaring was scary. Mr Popsicle, a good friend of ours, died on the crossings, he was hit by a cyclist maniac. He bumped his head so hard, he never got back up. The maniac cyclist just peered down at poor Mr Popsicle.'

Scamp adds. 'Ugh! Everyone ignored him. A kid gave him a foot shuffle and shifts him to the side of the curb. The cyclist looked at the prickly ball and sighed. He put his earplugs back in and pedalled off humming horrible music. Shortly after that, you saw us in shock only being guided by our sense of smell.'

Scotty says. 'Aye, thank goodness you made it across the gas-guzzling criss-cross maze. Both of you are safe now.'

HOMELESS MASCULUS!

The rip-roaring eruption explodes a booming noise. The chopping of trees from afar got so noisy that Masculus woke up from a well-deserved snooze.

The sweet-smelling pine trees made him relaxed and sleepy. Masculus stretches his arm, then pokes his little head out of his snug duvet. He grips his precious violin while he sleeps. He rubs his eyes and flops back to sleep. He is comfortable in his forever home, a wooden doll's house. Pansy and Lars, the neighbouring geese, hammer on Masculus' door. He ignores them and zonks out.

Masculus grumbles. 'Go away! Leave me alone!'

Lars shouts. 'Wake up!'

Masculus moans. 'I have a bow and arrow in the shape of a violin and bow-stick. I can aim as good as that Robin Hood, guy. I am a highly skilled archer and swords-mouse-man!'

Masculus squeals. 'Good night!'

Pansy utters. 'Huh! I bet that moping mouse has snuck back into bed still wearing his stupid Christmas pyjamas with matching hat.'

Lars shouts. 'The monster cutter is here!'

Masculus blubbers. 'Oh no, not again!'

Lars ushers. 'Yep, you've got it, little mouse. Get out of bed!'

Pansy blurts. 'We could do with a little ecowarrior help. Or you could opt for having your little biddy tail on the metal chopping board. Your violin will end up a pocket full of sawdust!'

Masculus wails. 'You and I aren't going to get along, goosy gander!'

Pansy explains. 'We have problems too. Our homes are covered in mushy plastics. We have flooding riverbanks, lakes, ponds and streams. The sea levels are rising every single day because of the extreme climate change. At least you had somewhere to hibernate.'

Masculus huffs. 'Listen, waddle-clogs, I lived on the leaky streets amongst burst water pipes. The flood barriers weren't strong enough to cope with the water pressures caused by the Antarctic's glacier melts. It's a good job I'm a nifty swimmer. The humans couldn't get into their homes either, because they were completely flooded out. They had to bail the water out with pots and pans.'

Pansy scowls. 'You, flea-bitten know-it-all rat face. I agree we are not going to get on.'

Masculus yells. 'I am not a rat! I'm a cornfield, village, city fish-and-chip shop, store-cupboard, attic mouse. My dolls' houses came with a digital door buzzer. The Mickey Mouse shoebox I used to reside belonged to a silly boy. He soon got fed up of me and put me in an old flower pot in the garden shed because his little sister was scared of mice. I even lived in a dog kennel and I hated it!'

Pansy chortles. 'Err. You mean the dog slavered its chops in your face.'

Masculus grits. 'Shut up you doddering geese-honking cluck!'

Lars clicks his tongue. 'Stop bickering. We have work to do. Like getting you out of bed!'

Masculus shrugs. 'Huh! Work? Me? I can't even flex a muscle right now. Give me a minute!'

Masculus slams the door shut and skids out, clutching his precious violin case.

Pansy replies. 'Try and flex your muscles collecting those little plastic toys you see at the caravan sites, surely you can manage that?'

Lars asks. 'Have you ever lived in one of those travelling caravans?'

Masculus sniffs. 'Nope, never-ever. Huh! I dread the thought of me and my violin being kicked to the curb for squatting.'

Lars remarks. 'With a strong name like Masculus,

you certainly are a wimpy mouse. Please be aware that we have bigger problems on the horizon than you!'

Pansy adds. 'The countryside looks as flat as a gigantic pancake. The monster cutter wants to create space for more rip-roaring entertainment. Come on, skedaddle and crack on.'

Masculus titters. 'Do ecowarrior chores make your palmate feet pong like sweaty socks?'

Pansy twists her bill. 'Rude!'

Masculus mopes. 'It's not fair! I'm not the working type. I've lived in warehouses fully packed with freshly baked egg-custard tarts. I'll miss those custard dives. You see, this mouse is more suited to the good life.'

Pansy gripes. 'There are worse things happening right now, Masculus. Now move it!'

Lars sighs. 'Remember Uncle Barnacle in the Antarctic? When he tried to visit us, he ended up in the wetlands in Firth, Scotland?'

Pansy grunts. 'Your point is?'

Lars answers. 'The glacier-melting crisis is everywhere. Uncle Barnacle will end up washed away if the water level keeps rising. Our Barnacle family will all be floating into the ocean pollution. And, he has been known to be a good diver.'

Masculus giggles. 'What's that got to do with the monster cutter?'

Pansy honks. 'Der. We will all end up homeless!'

DUCKY'S TIN POT TRAP!

Masculus hears a cry. 'Whose acting like a babbling-baby?'
  Pansy clucks. 'Oh. No! Ducky! We're over here! Look, it's us and the rude rodent.' Pansy waves her wings to draw Ducky's attention.

Lars stutters. 'Ducky! What in the blazes are you doing in the middle of a lake covered in metal gunge. How did you get in this predicament?'

Ducky sobs. 'I needed a cool paddle. I held up my banner, trying to get the tourists to read it without causing any fuss. I ended up in a tin-pot tussle. The tourists heckled me as if I was a comedy show.'

Masculus murmurs. 'Doofus Ducky waving a banner in the middle of toxic lakes, streams and rivers.'

Pansy clucks. 'Did you just mutter something, Masculus?'

Masculus fibs. 'It wasn't me. I must have a frog stuck in my throat. Argh!'

Pansy warns. 'If Ducky hears you, you're going to be the tussle in your own comedy show. Ducky will be heckling you!'

Pansy unties her pink lasso from around her slimline neck. She creates a noose for Ducky. She throws it towards his palmate feet. Lars decides to untie his green lasso as an extra life-saving aid. It takes a few attempts to yank Ducky out. The tug pulling is exhausting. The soaring heat makes it difficult as they grapple the high temperatures.

Masculus teases. 'Sorry, I'm not much help. My violin wasn't hand-crafted as a first-aid kit.'

Ducky chants. 'At last. I'm free!'

Masculus mimics. 'You've got whopping Duckzilla clogs. They would have been a fantastic paddle. And, we wouldn't have been bothered by you today.'

Ducky rasps. 'You try getting clonked on the head by the champagne-popping top maniacs followed by rusty love-locks!'

Pansy interjects. 'Ducky has been through an ordeal. It's not his fault his Duckzilla feet got stuck in a tin-pot lilypond. Oh! No! Ducky, forgive me for my rudeness.'

Ducky exhales. 'Mm. No comment.'

Lars shouts. 'We've got work to do! Professor MicroChip says: "Teamwork makes Dreamwork."'

Ducky says. 'Let's crack on!'

Masculus giggles. 'Those rusty love-locks must have given you a good clonking. I am certainly not in the mood for stupid chores!'

Ducky mumbles. 'There are tons of rubbish everywhere! Little mousey you really don't understand. Those fancy schmancy romancing champagne visitors go boating under the stars. Chucking this! Chucking that! I am waddling off to do my ecowarrior stint. See you later!'

FROGLIP'S METAL LILYPOND

Froglips enjoys the playful water lilies. She tries to dodge the sharp metal and wiry objects. She fails, now she's stuck on a metal water lily.

She glares at something strange in the water. It has clunks of metal shrapnel clanking around it. It bolts away into turbo-boost, she notices an odd-looking shell rattling and swirling backwards and forwards before it elevates into full force. It battles against the overspill pollution currents.

Froglips shouts. 'Oye!'

MissRed vaults. Boing! Boing! Boing! Along with the ocean algae gunge. She sloshes like a humungous ping-pong ball.

MissRed screams. 'Get me out of here!'

Froglips dumbfounds. 'Oooh! Are you an alien amphibian?'

MissRed gargles. 'Get me out of this chemical bondage, now!'

Froglips demands. 'What are you?'

MissRed splutters. 'I have no time to chitter-chatter. Help me!'

Froglips urges. 'Well, spit it out! What have you to say?'

MissRed screams. 'This is how you support a fellow water-creature?'

Froglips retorts. 'Sorry. I thought you were a deep-sea alien thing. You shot out from nowhere.'

'MissRed blurts. 'I think you're an alien amphibian with your plump red lips.'

MISSRED OCEAN TURTLE OIL-SLICK!

MissRed glugs. 'I'm a red-eared ocean turtle. I am covered in tidal wave-gunge. The currents and ocean-debris swamps the oceans every day. My lips are covered in oil-slick! I've got cotton buds stuck in my nostrils. The breaking sea waves and ocean-fills dragged me here. My beautiful face is unrecognisable.

Froglips probes. 'Do you have a name?'

MissRed mellows. 'Yes, MissRed.'

Froglips says. 'I'm not strong enough to save a hefty girl like you. I'll go and get some help.'

MissRed bleats. 'Please hurry.'

STAG'S FOSSIL FUEL FARTS

Froglips slithers away. Lars and Pansy waddle off to other sites. Froglips spots Stag in a tussle forcibly expelling air through his nostrils making powerful sneezes.

Froglips gasps. 'What happened to you?'

Stag grunts. 'I was minding my own business foraging in the forest. I stumbled into an oasis of broken razor-sharp glass bottles. I'm trapped! I need your help now!'

Froglips can't believe the weight of problems she's encountered. Stag gags heavily, so she suggests Stag sneezes to clear his nasal passage. He sniffs the air but the rise in methane gases creates an adverse effect. Stag isn't in a position to help MissRed. Froglips tries to remove the dangerous razor-sharp objects from around his hooves.

Froglips inflates her neck. 'Ouch! Oh, fiddle sticks! I've cut myself on sharp glass shards!'

Stag rasps. 'I'm not having much fun either. Go and get some help at once!'

Stag resumes burping and releasing smelly fossil-fuel farts from his butt-cheeks. The methane rises like a cloud around Froglips' face. Her eyes begin to stream with tears.

Froglips chokes. 'Icky! You stink really bad, Stag!'

Stag explains. 'I can't help it, can I? Human activity is to blame. It's all the burning fossil fuels, coal and oil releasing gases. It's not only polluting our environment but theirs too. Professor MicroChip says it can affect the atmosphere and cause climate change. Too much methane gases can harm Earth. With too much greenhouse gases, us wildlife are in danger from humans.'

Froglips croaks. 'Nothing new then?'

Stag continues. 'So sorry for not apologising in advance for my fossil-fuel inbuilt butt –blower, but let's face it, it was going to come out sooner rather than later.'

Froglips says. 'Yes. I understand what you're saying, but try not to flatulate in my face next time. I am wearing my best ruby red-lips, today.'

Stag apologises. 'Oopsy. Not again. Even worse, I'm trying to hold in my squeezy squits. I do hope we can still be besties.'

Froglips suggests. 'Try to aim away from my face. My red-lips are beginning to melt now!'

Stag continues. 'I've seen them burning fossil fuels in their fancy-schmancy, la-de-da, top-of-the-range mega-dosh barbecue grills and portable open-air ovens. The Prof says: "If the humans carry on, they'll make planet Earth sick, including us!"

Froglips adds. 'The Prof says humans have been seen offloading non-recyclable and recyclable chemical garbage on land that looks spacious, especially at night when it's dark and quiet. It's becoming a continuous cycle not to recycle.'

Stag grunts. 'Tons and tons of plastic packaging waste is piling up, some buried underground around our sites.'

Froglips hears footsteps snapping in the bushes and panics. 'Who's there? I'm not afraid of you. I'll tackle you with my hardwearing lily-pond shield. Put your hands up! Surrender now!'

Big Bro chuckles. 'Hi there, it's only me whooshing from behind the bushes.'

Froglips blurts. 'Oh, my goody-gum-drops, you gave me a giddy moment. What are you doing lurking behind the bushes?'

Big Bro explains. 'I'm looking for Little Bro. He took off on another adventure-seeking thrill this morning. As you know he misbehaves quite a lot and likes to snoop, hide and seek. Then, I met two pigs, Digby and Jax in distress. Then, along came two hedgehogs, Skipper and Scamp in a kerfuffle. As for Little Bro, I'll see him at The Recyclosaurus.'

Froglips croaks. 'I need your muscle power as a matter of urgency to help a red-eared ocean turtle. Right now, she's in a chemical waste bondage. Her name is MissRed. She says it's all down to the ocean-fill plopping dumpsters.'

    Stag is free. His strength is great for pulling. His teeth can unpick and untangle thick wiry objects.

    Stag scrambles out of the broken-glass trap.

    He sighs. 'Phew. Free at last!'

    Big Bro exhales. 'Ugh! Stag! You've just let off!'

    Froglips gags. 'He knows.'

    Stag chortles. 'I do apologise again, for this inconvenient gush of wind.'

Froglips cringes. 'Whoa! It, pongs!'

Stag gives his antlers a proper dusting down and his coat a mini-spring clean.

Froglips, Big Bro and Stag set off to save MissRed.

MissRed gargles. 'Argh! I see you took your time. The temperatures will get higher over time and more ocean-fills will turn into mass sea-gunge.'

Froglips blinks. 'What do you mean?'

MissRed bleats. 'I'm one of the lucky ones. Some sea creatures are washed away or buried in sand dunes on tropical beaches.'

Froglips says. 'I still don't know what you mean.'

MissRed hollers. 'Well, pout lips, I'm safe; my family are not. They have been eating plastic nurdles, mistaking them for wriggling colourful foods.'

Stag grunts. 'She means some of the ocean creatures have been poisoned, choked to death or buried on some beach flapping their fins or feet wriggling on shallow riverbanks.'

Froglips puffs. 'Ooh. I don't like the sound of that.'

Stag responds. 'No! I can't see you flapping your slithery arms or feet on any riverbank.'

MissRed gripes. 'This is not a laughing matter!'

Big Bro, Stag and Froglips untangle MissRed. Stag uses his huge grinding teeth and long tongue as a corkscrew. He works his way in and out of the wire mesh which was covering her beautiful red ears and decorative shell. Her red defining ocean turtle sculpture now looks prominent.

Froglips recalls. 'Rumour has it, the marine life fear for their lives because under the sea is nothing but contaminated water.'

MissRed replies. 'That's true. We can hardly taste the salt water now. Take those massive cruise liners, fancy yachts and other marine vessels, dumping their garbage into our ocean homes. We sea creatures are getting sicker because we can't tell what are our natural foods from the tiny pick-and-mixture plastics. Our happy place doesn't exist anymore.'

Froglips points. 'I don't know what we're going to do. The Prof says deforestation and ocean-fills is a huge problem. The woodland locations could be a recreation of the past one day. People may take their holidays under the deep seas. Or, exploring the possibility of holidays in outer space.'

MissRed yells. 'No! Not under the sea. Besides, if it's not fit for us then it won't be any use to the humans either!'

Froglips reassures. 'It was only a passing thought. Anyway, if the humans can turn our planet into a disaster zone, how would they treat another planet, if they got the chance to zoom up to outer space to live? I reckon the aliens would soon chuck them out!'

MissRed blathers. 'De-oceanfestation — or maybe "The ultimate human mish-mash de-outer-space-vacation." They'd soon run out of options; they could become homeless just like us!'

Froglips enquires. 'Does your head still hurt?'

MissRed hyperventilates. 'Yes. I am battered and bruised all over.'

Stag fusses. 'You can't get home by yourself. The ocean routes you took are danger zones now.'

Big Bro interjects. 'Professor MicroChip will call the dolphin pods to get her home safely. Maybe she could help with some chores.'

MissRed snivels. 'I'll do anything to get back home. That is, if I still have a home. I know cutting shards are swamping the waters. My tough shell can work as a carrier.'

THE SEAGULLS

Stag gallops to LA-LA Forest Park's Glamping Island resort. It boasts nothing less than exquisiteness. It has all top-of-the-range services and luxury amenities.

Stag boasts his fine torso to pose for the tourists. The demand for Stag on the family-album souvenir snaps make him a photoshoot celebrity.

Crowlip perches on a luxury yurt. The two doves, Annie and Polly observe.

Annie tweets. 'Mm. I know Stag gets private invites and quick selfie poses.'

Crowlip asks. 'Will I get an invite?'

Polly answers. 'I don't think so, with your snotty beak.'

Crowlip squawks. 'Rude!'

Polly bleats. 'Those huge yurts have strong posts supporting the extravagant crown roof in the shape of an ice-cream cone just like a circus tent with all the fangle-dangle trimmings. We perch for hours, spying, and waiting for the never-ending invites. We never get any invites. And, we are known to be the most elegant peace-loving birds.'

Crowlip tweets. 'Name-calling, peace-loving girly doves don't get invites.'

Pizza and Kebab click tongues. 'Mm. Strawberry and chocolate ice cream with candy sprinkles is sheer bird heaven.'

Polly reminds the gulls. 'It isn't an, "All you can eat birdy buffet." We have to bin those goodies!'

Annie tweets. 'Come on, girly gulls we have a lot of work to get through today. Be careful, dangerous sharp objects are buried in those sand dunes.'

The seagulls chatter. 'Hm. We're not cleaning those yurts. They have plenty more rooms than the others, including their own bathrooms, shower room, lounge and kitchen. The air-conditioner lobs us sideways. Huh! Let's not forget the bird-hating hounds!'

Polly nags. 'Yeah! You gulls have the perfect excuses. It's like, home-from-home for those tourists. Their beloved pets have jumping dog-paw imprints in the sand dunes. There's more stuff embedded in the sand than we realise.'

Annie tweets. 'Ooh. I don't think any of us should go there. It sounds like too many chores. Besides, those bow-wow dogs hate us.'

The gull's screech. 'Argh! Look at those bin liners bursting at the seams. Blah! Who's getting those chores!?'

Stag grunts. 'Not me, I am an A-list celebrity in demand.'

Polly chatters. 'Mm. More suited to those tittering magpies.'

Stag babbles. 'I'm the prime stud around these parts. I can't risk sticking my hooves into one of those disgusting bags. Ugh! I'll be out of a job!'

The magpies eavesdrop.

Perpetua moans. 'Cressida and I, have been over to those extravagant wood cabins with the bubbly tubs. There's more rubbish over that side than this side; it's more suited to the seagulls — they like a good old scavenge.'

The gulls scowl. 'We do chores! You nibble on stolen kibble nuts and milk cream!'

Crowlip jibbers. 'The more rubbish we collect the more treats we earn back at the secret garden.'

Perpetua and Cressida add. 'We can't blitz this tip. It's too much work. But we can round up some forest park animals to help us.'

Stag replies. 'That's what we're here for. It's called delegation.'

Perpetua overwhelms. 'Oh! What a smashing word.'

Cressida yammers. 'Mm. Delegation means

sharing the workload not scamming out of chores. I feel worn-out just thinking about slurping smooth cream from the doorstep milk-bottle tops.'

NASTY PATSY

Nelly canary tootles off to help look for Nay. She elevates along the riverbanks before venturing deeper into the woodlands. She decides to take a break. Nelly stirs the murky water with her beak before taking a sip from the river to quench her thirst. She sees a comfortable tree stump to perch on. Her feathers are stuck to a gungy plastic bag. She tries to yank herself away from tree stump. Nelly struggles and hits the ground headfirst.

She cries. 'Ouch!'

Nelly tries to flutter but her wings have lost power. She takes tippy claw trots and hears howling shock waves run down her spine.

Nasty Patsy froths. 'Ooh. I see a flash of vibrant yellow, who could this be? Oh. It's my, Little Nelly jelly-belly.'

Nelly quivers. 'I may have a yellow belly, but I'm not scared of you anymore!'

Patsy snarls. 'Oye! I will take great pleasure kicking your little butt! Not so brave now, Nell Bells?'

The gulls perch high on the conifer tree nearby. Nelly's ordeal is witnessed by Pizza, Kebab, Hotdog, Fish and Chips.

Nelly struggles. 'You've set boobytraps all over the place for me.'

Patsy's drips stringy froth. 'Of course!'

Nelly dodges. 'Leave me alone!'

Patsy scrunches her nose. 'I'm going to eat you. Shut your little beaky clap-trap!'

Nelly pleads. 'Please don't eat me. I taste awful. I've been munching on slimy rotten slugs today.'

The seagulls found balancing difficult. They had just had a hearty feast at the posh sites and have eaten too much junk foods from another site.

Patsy sniffs. 'Back off! You pesky pot-bellied thieving flying rat-bats!'

Kebab scolds. 'Rude!'

Patsy giggles. 'Whose been mimicking kittens today, trying to lure the tourists into your trap, so you can scoop on them and grab whatever you can!'

Chips gargles. 'How dare you call us flying rat-bats!'

Patsy smirks. 'News flash: "Beware! Pesky seagulls purr like kittens perching on house roof tops. They love wheeling and dealing and enjoy stealing. They take it in turns to spread their germs and diseases."

The gulls chatter. 'There's a lot of deforestation taking place everywhere. Our forest and woodlands are getting smaller and soon there'll be none! What are we to do? There's not enough natural food source to go round. We were here first!'

Patsy growls. 'So was I!'

The gulls justify. 'Well. We reckon the grub is on offer for the swooping.'

Patsy laughs. 'Nice try. I heard a rumour: You gulls flew to the Glamping Island Resort, trying out the latest menus. Left-over cheesy pineapple pepperoni pizzas, mouth-watering kebabs, fish and chips and let's not forget the hotdogs.'

The gulls squawk. 'Fibber!'

Patsy hisses. 'You bad girls should be doing chores. I'm going to snitch. What will Professor bullseye say? Mm. Send you all to Bird BootCamp where you will be fed on tasteless rotten scavenger leftover grub!'

Hotdog blurts. 'You're bluffing!'

Chips bleats. 'Liar, liar, your bum-cheeks on fire!'

Pizza shouts. 'Humbug!'

Kebab rasps. 'How dare you suggest we steal!'

Fish cringes. 'You can't prove it.'

Patsy taunts. 'Whose been pinching all the happy-go-lucky children's meal deals. I suppose you eat the dinky plastic toys as well?'

The seagulls debate. 'How did Patsy find out? Didn't we destroy all the evidence? Oh! No! If, BirdCop finds out, then it's definitely Bird BootCamp for us! Blah! With no return!'

Chips tweets. 'I know, we gave those plastic toys a swift claw-kick to the curb!'

Hotdog chews. 'Jog on, feisty fox!'

Patsy spits. 'You belching scoundrels!'

Hotdog burps. 'Oops. Pardon me. Birds don't eat or hide plastic toys.'

Patsy tucks in her tail and pins her ears back. The electrifying fur along her spine stands prominent.

She growls. 'You, conniving scavenging rogues. You won't get away with this!'

The gulls freeze to a standstill. Patsy shows off her fine sculpture. She chillingly tramples around.

Kebab distracts. 'We have a busy day with chores. We bid you goodbye!'

Seagulls parade full plumage as they attempt to flutter off.

Nelly jumps. 'Can we go now?'

Patsy gnashes. 'I will keep Nelly as a tasty hostage, if that's okay.'

Seagulls reason: 'That would be very foolish. Your misfortune is that you are stout and strong and have innate hunting abilities. You don't know how to use your talents very well which makes you a big fat bully. We're natural flying hunters and in return our natural environment should provide enough food for all of us.'

Kebab chirps. 'Obviously, things haven't worked out as nature planned.'
Patsy claws her chin.
She hisses. 'Shut up you blithering idiots!'
The seagulls crisscross between hidden branches. They clasp Nelly with their long claws. Her wings have packed up. The injury makes her body difficult to elevate to safety.

Patsy snarls:

"Burp. Nelly Canary tasty food starter,
Golden slurp soup of the day,
Now, Little Yellow jelly belly has gone away.
Belch. Flying podgy rat-bat gulls,
Pizza, Kebab, Fish, Chips and Hotdog,
Delicious main course bird stew hot-pot."

A R Trent

They all freeze to a standstill, hoping the bully falls asleep out of boredom. Fish rants. 'Even better, back off!'
Nelly blubbers. 'I'm going to die, right here, right now.'
Little Bro, Ed and Emee hear little Nelly in distress. They dash towards her cries and witness Nasty Patsy terrorising her.
Patsy spits. 'Who's going to protect you now, Tweety-heart?'

Ed shouts. 'Stop bullying her!'

Patsy snorts. 'Well, well. What have we here? A dirty school brat!'

Ed challenges. 'We mean you no harm. We're not dangerous. And, by the way, I'm not dirty.'

Patsy growls. 'Liar! Liar! Your trouser britches are on fire!'

Ed frowns. 'Rude!'

Little Bro interjects. 'We must crack on with our chores so we will bid you farewell. Come on Ed, Nelly and Gulls. Let's scarper!'

Patsy hisses. 'What? No fun nor feast! No scrawny boy introduction?'

Ed answers. 'Oh. My name is Ed Williams, I'm ten-years of age.'

Patsy remarks. 'Huh! Filthy hands! I see you sprogs stuffing your faces, littering our woodlands, food fighting, wiping your sweaty heads and snot-dribbling noses with your hands! You, dirty, dirty, boy!'

Ed remarks. 'I have to agree with you, some kids in my school have smelly hands because they don't wash them properly. Ugh! Some kids wipe their snotty noses on their school jumpers.'

Patsy sniffs. 'Blah!'

Ed reiterates. 'I wash my hands every day. My grandad taught me at an early age. Look! I'm wearing biodegradable gloves. Little Bro gave me these for ecowarrior chores. So, don't pick on me!'

Little Bro chants. 'Ed carries hand-sanitizing gel.'

Patsy demands. 'Give me, that jelly-wash now!'

Ed laughs. 'You can't use hand gel. You don't have hands. You have dirty sharp claw-like nails to bully little birds, don't you?'

Patsy hisses. 'I'm going to scratch your button nose, you filthy boy!'

Emee tries to protect Ed. She elevates her kangaroo jumps. Her back legs now show her white fluffy paw socks. The white diamond-shape on her chest is now prominent. She glares at Patsy. She boasts her wide-open jaw and sharp gnashers, she flares her staffy nostrils with aggression and fight!

Emee growls. 'Roar! Grr!'

Patsy takes a backward stumble into a prickly cactus plant.

Patsy yelps. 'Ouch! Aww! My beautiful butt-cheeks stings. You little scruffy mutt!'

Little Bro enquires. 'Where did you learn to kangaroo jump like that?'

Emee yaps. 'My previous owner had a sniffling little nuisance boy. That kind man taught me to do tricks to make the kid laugh, before I was dognapped.'

The chitter-chatter halts. A jagged wire mesh sheet flew from nowhere wedging underneath Emee's back legs.

Patsy spits. 'Gotcha! Not the leader of the pack hounds now, are you?'

Ed shouts. 'You're a nasty piece of work!'

Patsy grins. 'Nasty is my name, don't wear it out.'

Nelly quivers, 'Why do you love to bully?'

Patsy snarls. 'Why not?'

Little Bro struggles to untangle Emee, from the wiry mesh.

Emee yelps. 'Both my back legs are stuck!'

Ed makes another attempt to connect to his digital assistance, YO. Nasty Patsy sees Ed twiddling his thumbs on his phone.'

Patsy circles. 'What's that? Give it to me!'

Ed shouts. 'No! And, you can stop the snarling drop-spits. You're the one that stinks around here. Blah!'

Patsy huffs. 'What did you say, Wimpy boy?'

Ed sings: 'Ding-a-ling-a-dong. Nasty Patsy pinga-pongs.'

Little Bro ushers Ed. 'Bruv, it might be a good idea to shut your pie-hole now. She's not backing down and, I don't feel brave enough to save you.'

Patsy hisses. 'I am going to hunt you all down. You'll make good sport for me!'

Emee woofs. 'Doofus boy!'

MAGPIE TURBO POOPS!

Cressida and Perpetua hover around scanning their beady eyes on the lookout. They hear troubling voices echoing high-pitched fear.

Perpetua blurts. 'Surprise, surprise, that horrid creature from the swampy side is on her bullying spree again. Let's swoop over to have a look.'

Patsy seethes. 'Ugh! This is all I need right now, two creepy magpies!'

Cressida chatters. 'Glad to make your acquaintance too, trout lips!'

Patsy scoffs. 'Back-off! Mind your own business. Don't you have somewhere to go? You know, slurping cream from milk bottle tops?'

Little Bro cautions. 'Just ignore her. We have chores to be getting on with.'

Patsy snaps. 'Leave the dirty schoolboy to me. I'll deal with him and his grubby hands. I'll nip at his skinny fingers first!'

Ed remarks. 'I've already told you my hands are clean. Grandad says: "Cover your coughs, cover your sneezes. They can airborne travel. Use a clean tissue so it doesn't spread diseases.'

Patsy hisses. 'Grandad says this! Grandad says that! You are a headache!'

Ed replies. 'I've never been called a headache before.'

Robby pops his head from behind the shrubs. 'Err. Hm. I was just wondering if anyone had seen my little sister, Nay. She hopped off some time ago. She's nowhere to be seen.'

Patsy salivates. 'Burp! That rabbit stew was tasty!'

Robby objects. 'Err. Nay wouldn't taste very nice. Her palate only prefers slugs and snails and the odd stinky rat tail.'

Patsy sniffs. 'I don't believe you. That ball of fluff only took one gulp. Num. Num. I didn't whiff any slithery bugs or slugs or rodent tail.'

Nelly wails. 'Hop off, Robby! Oopsy. I forgot you can't hop!'

Robby shrieks. 'No, Nelly. I can't hop but I can sprint as fast as a cheetah in the jungle.'

Nelly sniffles. 'Why do you have to be so cruel, Patsy?'

Patsy attempts to pounce on Robby. Perpetua squawks. 'Leave them alone! We are fully loaded with shocking turbo poops!'

Patsy quibbles. 'Then poop off! I can't deal with you right now! I am far too busy with this lot!'

Cressida chuffs. 'Patsy you are in for a raucous surprise!'

Magpies titter. 'Ready! Aim! Fire! Get your free turbo turds Patsy! Try these stinky loops for size, These bad boys come in various shapes and sizes and right now, the bullseye is you!'

The magpies hurl their turbo poops on Patsy's well-groomed soft fur , sploshing in her ears, down her cheeks, trickling droplets into her mouth.

Patsy complains. 'You will perish. It'll be me plopping you all out of my foxy potty bottom!'

Nelly tweets. 'Stop!'

Patsy nitpicks. 'Don't you all forget that your new friend is a human. We're all homeless because of him!'

Ed felt he was now in the spotlight for trouble.

Patsy brags. 'Got anything to say, boy?'

Ed blurts. 'Well, I saw a homeless baby deer. The fawn was jumping over my garden hedge. It trotted along pathways scrambling around the neighbourhood with the others.'

Patsy scowls. 'What did I say? It's his fault!'

Ed blurts. 'Why do I, have to take all the blame?'

Patsy grins. 'He may be a little boy but he's still a human litter-lout on a killing voyage. Let's all agree, Ed is a liar!'

Little Bro yells. 'No! Don't blame Ed for mass pollution! He's just a ten-year-old lost boy. He's on the eco-campaign with us. He's got a box full of plastic bottles and cans left by the tourists. He's a proper ecowarrior just like us. Patsy is looking for someone to blame. She's having her own jolly funday by picking on Ed. Don't, believe her.'

The magpies respond. 'Here we go again! Ready! Aim! Fire! Don't miss her trout-pout. Take that, from Ed!'

Patsy cowers. 'Not again!'

Nelly chirps. 'What about the seagulls? Maybe they've been to the deli posh sites. Wow! They'll have more than just junk food sloppy poops for Nasty Patsy.'

Perpetua chortles. 'Don't rely on those gulls, Nelly.'

Patsy scarpers. 'I'll be coming back for you. Just you wait and see!'

Perpetua and Cressida tweets. 'Does anyone sniff gulls wafting through the putrid air? BirdCop and Bossy Blute are on the prowl for greedy birds.'

Cressida inspects. 'Hey gulls! We can smell your burps from miles away. We managed to scare away gangster Patsy without you.'

Hotdog screeches. 'Please don't snitch. Bird BootCamp doesn't appeal to us.'

Fish blubbers. 'The truth is, our claws haven't done any chores today. We left Nelly with Nasty Pasty. We didn't protect her.'

Hotdog blurts. 'The magpies saved Nelly.'

Kebab bickers. 'Mm. They prefer bottles over cartons. They steal too. And, we get dubbed the rummaging disease-ridden flying rat-bats.'

Perpetua eavesdrops. 'Patsy nearly ate Nelly today because you gulls were out scrumping for junk food. You will be carted off to Bird BootCamp, the infamous No Birds Land if you get found out.'

Chips rants. 'Don't say that word, that one-way ticket to Bird BootCamp with no return. We couldn't grab Nelly because our bellies were too podgy. The Bird BootCamp sea creatures would leave us their floating rotten dredged up creepy crawly scraps. Blah! We would need our own supply of sick-bags!'

Hotdog blurts. 'Get me a sick-bag now!'

Pizza puffs. 'Huh! Only if BirdCop and Blute crime squad catches us.'

Kebab huffs. 'They won't catch us.'

Fish chuffs. 'Well girls, it's about time we seagulls went on a healthy diet and did some honest chores.'

The seagulls disperse, scanning for any light-weight recyclable sharp objects.

THE RECYCLOSAURUS

The EggBangers and ecowarriors assemble.
Professor MicroChip debates:
'The visitors have flocked in their thousands to LA-LA Forest Park, bringing personal belongings, electrical and non-electrical items to scatter on our grounds. This park is now an entertainment extravaganza. It offers unlimited exquisite luxury amenities. The site homes hundreds of accommodations. Sorry to say, supply and demand works for them. Our already fragile woodlands and forest parks are on the verge of collapse. Deforestation is an ongoing project for the larger structural demands by tourists wanting holiday breaks. This means the construction monster cutters are at large.'

Blute rounds up the ecowarriors: 'Stand to attention!'

Blute flutters onto Professor MicroChip's shoulder, dodging the USB connectors.

Blute announces. 'As you are aware, I am the only bird scientist in the whole world. I am expecting good results: no excuses, collection perfection and a spic-and-span mission.'

Blute asks Max. 'Where's my garden sparrow spy, Ozzy? I am looking forward to the local neighbourhood gossip.'

Max answers. 'Erm. Well, as usual Ozzy tweets me at dawn. He says, the air pollution is stinky, all the people are walking, talking and farting at the same time. The greenhouse gas effect isn't just affecting our wildlife but theirs too. The humans sometimes fly-tip in their own gardens, doorsteps and on the pavements.'

Blute replies. 'Thank you, for the newsflash. I know your brother Ozzy is more than just a nosey parker around the local gardens; and he's more calamity accident prone than you are.'

Max chirps. 'Ozzy says you're too superior to get your bird-scientist claws clogged up with poop. My brother also says I'm a super-snitch.'

Blute gawps. 'Rocky Robin, I hope you were grafting with Ozzy and Max in the neighbourhoods.'

Rocky tweets. 'Yes sir. Your Royal Highness Scientist. I lost sight of Ozzy early this morning. I did spot him having a little snooze on ground level. Mm. He did seem a little zonked out.'

Max interjects. 'Ozzy was stalking a juicy curly whirly worm. He took a deep ground dive to pluck it up. I thought he squawked: "Help!"

Blute huffs. 'And you – did what?'

Max snickers. 'I left him.'

Rocky cackles. 'I think, he caught the juicy curly whirly worm.'

Blute probes. 'He either did, or he didn't. Which one is it?'

Max gibbers. 'Don't ask me. I wasn't there.'

BirdCop squawks. 'Rocky, you do know about Bird BootCamp, don't you?'

Rocky gargles. 'Well, maybe he wasn't having a little snooze. Or maybe he was. And yes, I do know about Bird BootCamp and its special grubby diets.'

HANDSOME THE OWL

Blute checks. 'Handsome, I hope you've been keeping a watchful eye?'
 Handsome hoots. 'Ter-twit-ta-ooh, most definitely, King Blute.'
Blute asks. 'Spill the beans, Handsome. Do you have any concerns that need discussing at The Recyclosaurus today?'
Handsome moots. 'The notorious teeth gnashing Nasty Patsy has been up to her old tricks again. She thought Nelly would be a delicious recipe for her bird-soup starter.'
Blute blinks. 'Huh! Goody gum-drops, I'm glad she changed her mind.'
Handsome observes. 'The local school is closed due to the extreme weather conditions. A schoolboy took this as a hint to seek a thrilling adventure and missed his school bus on purpose. He broke his mobile phone by getting slaps on the back from the notorious school bully. He got more cut-slaps and was forced to act as a leap-frog for the school cronies. He hid from the school caretaker behind the nearest tree before wandering off into LA-LA Forest Park to get himself lost. He seemed to be in a state of: "happy to be lost rather than in total shock." His ham-and-cheese-pickle sandwich was stalked by a runaway scruffy Staffy

dog and our drip-snot Crowlip. The local dog prison warden is on the lookout for the mutt. I regret to inform you that our nearest and dearest EggBanger, Little Bro, is partner in crime. I believe they'll be arriving soon, at The Recyclosaurus.'

Blute goes into a head spasm. His green specs now lob-sided down his face.

'Oh. Deary me. How can losing oneself be fascinating, and what's the runaway stray dog story?'

Handsome assesses. 'The Staffy is indeed a dog-escapologist. The dog warden has been on the hunt to take her back to the Dog Rescue Centre. She legged it like a kangaroo maniac from their kennels. Emee has been collecting doggy poop bags and dog food tins from the sites. She's done a brilliant job and has impeccable toilet manners. Ed has been an excellent ecowarrior collecting dangerous cutting bottles and tin cans in a recyclable green box.'

Ed, Emee and Little Bro arrive late. They snoop in on the tail-end of the conversation.

Crowlip hovers. 'Oopsy. I think I'm in trouble.'

Emee yaps. 'I'm the best dog-escapologist around these parts. It takes a steady nerve to be this good and with utmost bravery.'

Ed, interjects. 'What do you mean, Emee?'

Emee barks. 'I know when to act fast!'

Ed laughs. 'My sandwich must have slowed you down when you were squabbling with Crowlip over my ham-and-cheese-pickle sandwich.'

Blute ponders. 'Mm. Maybe the Prof will be lenient with Little Bro. I know for sure, abandoning any child or dog in this unimaginable heat would be unforgiveable. Little Bro, mischievous you are; heart of gold you certainly have.'

Ed prods. 'I got lost to get ideas for my school project.'

Blute suggests. 'Mm. Handsome has a poem. You might all learn something from it.'

Ed stutters. 'Err. Okay. I'll have a listen.'

Handsome hoots:

"I rotate my round wise old head,
I can fly like the speed of light,
I see and hear, I am a talker rather than a doer,
The less I speak, the more I hear,
I sit courageously like an old Oak tree,
Birds flock to perch on brittle parched branches,
Our woodland looks grimmer, flowers dimming drier,

The heated wildfires get higher, bird travel choirs are lost in song,
Planet Earth slowly transforms into a monumental burning wreck,
Tickety-boo! Land and ocean-fill dumpsters whoosh!'
Stag grunts: 'My butt-cheek is like a fossil-fuel gas air-filler.'
The Glaciers are melting, there's no place for ocean life slayers,
MissRed cries: 'Toxic rubbish endangers all sea creatures.'
Nay blubbers: 'Get me out, of this plastic bag! You, litter-critter-killers.'
Robby shouts: 'Climate Change Kills. Let's act now to reduce it!'
Froglips croaks: 'This is not my tin-can-lilypond. Recycle it!'
Ducky quacks: 'Ouch! Keep your rusty love-locks to yourself!'
Greg thrills: 'Hey there tourists! My, Plan B, Planet Friendly Bag will teach you a good lesson, it's free of charge.'
Humans say: 'We've got the solution. We know best.'
'Sounds like the new devolution, not a modern world evolution.
Your, Great-great-great, great grandchildren will inherit Earth,
This will not be a quick-fix suture or buckaroo hired-hand worker.
Climate Change is in the frame. Oh. Yes, you are to blame!'
Unborn historians will say: 'Our dome home is no fun; we can't see the sun.
Ancestors say: "What have we done?"

A R Trent

Blute halts. 'Thank you Handsome for your future remote viewing.'

Handsome replies. 'Twit-ta-ooh, Sir Blute.'

Blute sighs. 'Late as usual my seagulls. I hope you haven't been on a scoffing spree today?'

Seagulls stammer. 'Good day, Halloo, Howdy, Hi, How-do-you-do.'

Pizza huffs. 'Before you probe us, we haven't been at the Posh Sites today. Yuk! Those posh deli counters pong like a pair of reeking cheesy socks.'

Blute prods. 'Mm. Lots of takeaway hot and cold foods around LA-LA Forest Park up for grabs. You gulls do not have the willpower to turn the other beak.'

Greg warns. 'Be aware: some of the packaging is made from dangerous toxic chemicals. It spreads its molecules into the air.'

Seagulls blurts. 'Oh! No! We may have ingested some of the plastic killing chemicals!'

Blute suspects. 'You all seem to be alive and kicking. What another whopping lie. You smell of junk and posh food deli scraps, again!'

The gull's quiver. 'Oh! Please! Not the Bird BootCamp discussion again!'

Blute warns. 'This is your final warning!'

BLUTE BIRD SCIENTIST

Blute explains. 'The humans say our gulls are addicted to junk food. They are greedy scavenging tubby rat-bats spreading germs and diseases. Gulls need to curb their greedy habits!'

The gulls kept a stiff upper-bill. 'Yes Captain Blute, we will behave in future!'

Blute affirms. 'Those outlaw fly-tippers seem to know when they are going to be busted! It looks like they secretly scan the sites when Park Ranger, Kane, isn't on duty. They off-load the foreign wastes wherever deemed possible without being spotted! The humans are spreading diseases too.'

Stag grunts. 'The gulls find scavenging ground level more appealing, gouging their bills with grub rather than litter picking. Let's not forget, Nelly might have been Patsy's delicious bird-soup starter. The pot-bellied gulls were unable to save her today.'

Fish splutters. 'Rude!'

Chips squawks. 'Stag, I always thought you had a snitch-face!'

Rocky interjects. 'Can I just say, we thought the migrating birds took Nay. Now we know it was gangster, Nasty Patsy.'

Handsome twirls. 'The extreme weather conditions have made you all befuddled. And, as for tyrant Patsy, munching on a little rabbit would be the least of her problems. I hear she scarpered off somewhere. The migration birds were already confused. The smell of greenhouse-gas fumes has affected us all. The majority of the migration birds took flight somewhere else leaving a handful of birds roaming. They won't find any sweet exotic grubs around these parts or anywhere decent to perch or rest.'

Blute gasps. 'Oh, doodle-doo, what shall I do with them? I cannot give them chores because they are in a right old tizzy.'

Stag grunts. 'A young muntjac was seen wandering around jumping garden fences and hedges in the front and back gardens nearby. Mm. They often sleep in the shrubberies. They have nowhere to go; their natural habitats are occupied by newly built flats for people to live in.'

Masculus meddles. 'Oh! You don't say!'

Citrus twists his orange bill. 'Good day to you, Mister Professor Chipsy. We have found ourselves in a jar of pickled mango. Magenta and I got lost in song. We followed the foolish migration bird choir.'

Magenta plumages. She swings her dainty, cerise-coloured bag. 'Could you please point us in the right direction to Jamaica? May I say, these parts stink worse than old Citrus' jazzy razzamatazz socks after he's been jiving all night in the hot sun.'

Citrus responds. 'Magenta, my sweetness, you took a shine to that skinny diddly one-foot pigeon carrier who cracked his head on a wind turbine.'

Magenta felt techy. 'That one-foot charming pigeon seemed to know his way around these parts.'

Citrus fusses. 'Mm. Huh. Magenta, he took a fancy to your flashing beady eyes. He was the favourite to win. Hm. Huh! That show-off skinny one-foot pigeon loop-de-looped around the wind turbine before bucking his head to ground level!'

Magenta retaliates. 'Hush your beak. I am not in the mood for your foolishness today.'

Citrus moots. 'Professor Micro Chipsy, it has been a very long confusing journey. We followed the racing pigeons to disaster and now we need your help to get home.'

Magenta adds. 'Citrus found them quite amusing. He stalked that one-foot pigeon. Mm. He was gripping the hundred-to-one betting slip. It floated towards Citrus in a whooshing gush of wind. Old Citrus likes to back a winner. Back home he prances on top of the ripe mangoes.

He beats his wings behind his bird-butt-cheeks up and down with his feathery fingertips towards the winning line.'

Citrus coos. 'Mm. Huh. My new pigeon pal came swooping across the tree-tops towards me today. The daft one-foot pigeon nearly dropped my lucky betting slip. I watched it twirl away. Mm. Huh. I saw that pigeon perform acrobatics in the air between the spikey metal giant. He disappeared splat on the ground.'

Magenta puffs. 'That stupid betting slip fell amongst the filthy pile of slops.'

Citrus huffs. 'Another racing pigeon bolted towards my betting slip. He clasped it, then dropped it into another overspill dumpster full of more slops smothered in flies. It smelt worse than my jazzy razzamatazz smelly socks. Goodness me, all I saw was betting slips raining from the heavens.'

Magenta flaps. 'You'd better stick to racehorse betting because we don't want you to end up like that dead one-foot pigeon, idiot.'

Citrus notes. 'We did meet two most charming migration birds, Piérre and Anushka. Piérre couldn't sing, never mind join a migrating bird choir. It's no wonder he got himself lost.'

Magenta interjects. 'Well, they certainly didn't want to come with us. The seasons are bamboozling us migration birds. There's no such thing as a tropical wintry January.'

Professor MicroChip explains. 'The birds flutter around the wind turbines and end up in bird heaven. Those wind turbines are energy efficient. Bird deaths are unintentional as the energy helper burns less carbon monoxide in the atmosphere. The humans are trying to rely on natural resources like wind power for fuel.'

Pansy notices. 'Blute, you don't have much to say.'

Lars intrudes. 'Why, should birds die from those windy things? I am not trying to ruffle your blue fluffy feathers, but a bird of your high calibre should know everything. Afterall, you are the only bird scientist in the whole world.'

Blute squawks. 'Didn't you hear the Prof? Are you calling me stupid?'

Lars cringes. 'You are the only clever dicky-bird scientist in the whole wide world, I wouldn't dare back-chat you.'

Blute blurts. 'The perils of plastic and air-fuel contamination will affect every living being, including human beings, marine and ocean life, wildlife and land animals including the plant kingdom. I feel giddy-doo-lally now. I need a quiet perch.'

Stag chomps. 'When are we eating? I'm exhausted from those demanding touristy hot-shot picture postcards.'

Froglips prods. 'You love the exit entrance posing-picture snaps.'

Stag whispers. 'You can't be serious. Sloppy poops stuck in my hooves! Broken glass bottles and getting wired to the knees. Huh! They think I'm a stud; I'm an unpaid stag!'

Blute utters. 'Did you say anything, Stag?'

Stag answers. 'Err. It's a good job the wind turbines are not ground level. I can't picture myself hanging onto a propeller wing whizzing around like a frisbee.'

Prof MicroChip says. 'The humans view wind turbines as a natural source of energy without spilling out further pollution into the air. A hundred-thousand bird species are killed including migration birds. Climate change worldwide outweighs the damage to our planet because it is rapidly and silently burning up. The future of the natural world hangs in the balance. We wildlife see the humans as a big threat. We believe the EggBangers, Recyclosaurus and ecowarriors can make a difference by slowly reversing the damages caused.'

Bionca points. 'What will the humans do in two or three hundred years' time when there's nowhere for them to live?'

Bizzy says. 'Erm. They started this war a very long, long, time ago.'

Froglips croaks. 'Well, I would like to take this opportunity to say, I had to put up with Stag's flatulating farts! The aroma was so intoxicating my red-lipstick started to melt down my chin.'

Stag adds. 'It explains the fog and soot fossil-fuel issues, Froglips. As for your trout-pout, I do apologise. I hope we still can be besties.'

Prof recaps. 'The top air pollutants are affecting the Earth and the wildlife. Most air pollution comes from energy use, and production. For instance, driving a car on petrol, heating a home with oil, running a power plant on fracked gas etc. Fossil fuel is burnt and harmful chemicals and gases are released into the air. Smog is built up by increasing heat and, when the weather gets to extreme heat, more ultraviolet radiation occurs. In addition, climate change increases the production of allergenic air pollutants, including mould. The mouldy damp conditions again are caused by extreme weather. The worse scenario is increased flooding, even higher pollen levels due to a longer pollen season.'

Citrus coos. 'Mm. Huh!'

MissRed complains. 'I am not invisible. What about the sea creatures like me?'

Prof answers. 'Oh. We'll have to come back to the ice-melts later.'

Masculus frowns. 'I escaped from the wicked monster cutter today! And I've lived on loads of leaky streets.'

Prof explains. 'Traffic exhaust is exceptionally toxic together with the wildfire smoke. More and more chopping trees day-by-day and wildfire is widespread. Many of you will inhale the campfire smoke and portable barbecue-fuel-burning grills. All these factors are polluting the air; not only Stag will experience the, "Oopsy, I'm so sorry for my farts" but the rest of you will be breaking butt-wind power and burps in due course.'

MissRed sniffles. 'I am not supposed to be here. I am a heavily armoured reptile with a bony shell to cover my ribs, back and underneath my body. It should give me extra protection. My predator is mass ocean-fill pollution. My pace and agility are limited on land. I don't have teeth but

I have a sharp horny beak. This allows me to eat because I can break up food on land or sea.'

Pansy yawns. 'And, your point is?'

Lars butts in. 'MissRed couldn't protect herself this time. Her heavily armoured inbuilt padding was completely covered in metal wiry stuff and she had two straws stuck in her nostrils.'

Pansy giggles. 'Lars' heart is beating with love for MissRed.'

Lars honks. 'It's not funny! She's eaten plastic nurdles. She's covered in oil-slick and has sharp nails sticking into her beautiful neck!'

Ducky quacks. 'I got caught up in pile of tin cans with sharp edges, plastics and metals. I was clonked on my head by those falling rusty love-locks!'

Froglips croaks. 'Mm. We know about you getting clonked.'

BirdCop shushes. 'Ed, will return to school and start his project on: "Extreme Climate Change – the Cause and Effect."

Prof says: "Do your research."

Ed interjects. 'Err. Mm. I will try my best to spread the word about climate-change. Erm. And, I won't be chaining myself to monumental buildings or anything like that. I certainly won't be causing a massive unfriendly fuss to get my point across. That's all I would like to say right now. Please don't pick on me because I am a human. I do recycle a lot.'

Professor MicroChip adds. 'Plastics are important to the humans because they rely on these materials. For instance for: clothing, computers, furniture, even body parts that are necessary but used one time only. Plastic packaging is made from dangerous chemicals that cannot be recycled – bottles and plastic carrier bags of all sizes etc. These plastic bags are the world's biggest polluters.'

Ed exhales. 'It's not my fault!'

Prof continues. 'The humans have a phrase, "Plastic Oceans." Around five-hundred-billion plastic bags are used every year. A lot of the plastic bags are used for maybe, four to five minutes. Nay got stuck in a filthy plastic bag today; Bizzy and Bionca rescued her. The horse's hate windy plastic bags. Greg has produced a super-duper Plan B, bag for life made from Earth's natural resources.'

Greg feels bashful. 'Oh. It's just something I mustered up.'

Scotty larks. 'Aye, Greg.'

Prof adds. 'Most plastics are reusable. Unfortunately, they are dumped in landfills and ocean-fills. Poor MissRed munches on a lot of living organism foods but also ingests invisible microplastic nurdles. Animal food has plastic bits too. Just imagine plastic bottles in the ocean – the seawater and sunlight make the plastics brittle. The bottles start to degrade and they crumble into pieces of molecules that become even smaller and tinier. The microplastics can take about four-hundred and fifty-years to degrade in the ocean.'

MissRed blurts. 'Seabirds, crabs, squids and other sea creatures will eat coloured plastics too.'

Seagulls interrupt. 'We are eating poor quality foods. Are we going to die!'

MissRed squeals. 'That's nearly every ocean life in the sea! I got swallowed up by a 'mighty whumpf!' The avalanches whoosh and blanket our waters which are homes to us. It's not fair!'

Lars huffs. 'Hm. All this talk is upsetting MissRed.'

Ed adds. 'I will try my best to do my part to save Planet Earth.'

Skipper interrupts. 'We like water, don't we, Scamp?'

Scamp replies. 'Oh, yes, we do. We like to loop-de-loop in the shallow streams.'

Masculus frowns. 'You stupid hoglets. What's that got to do with ocean-fills and rising water levels?'

Skipper answers. 'Nothing really, apart from it being water.'

Masculus snoops. 'Your Uncle Barnacle is battling with ice melts.'

Lars explodes. 'Okay! Now we are on the water issues again. Nosey Masculus heard Pansy and me talking about our Barnacle family. They used to travel by flight and land rest. They would end up in their many thousands on Solway Firth in Scotland. They ate all winter on the salt-flats and marshes. The Wildlife Trust Reserve was ideal for them. We hope they have the sense to stay where they are because it doesn't feel like winter right now.'

Prof says. 'Barnacles are small migratory geese that flutter to Northern Britain. The wintry wetlands draw them in. There are thousands of them migrating in their own preferred numbers. Over the recent decades they have become increasingly popular and are being seen at nearly all the wetlands in any season. And yes, the Barnacles do the yapping calls and like to go into calling song and chorus with each other.'

Scotty interjects. 'Aye. It's not a good idea to travel right now, especially when some migration birds are feeling weather-giddy and forgetting their songs.'

Citrus jests. 'Mm. Huh. Them icy migration birds mustn't come here for a family visit. They'll end up forced to take a dive into one of those fancy champagne ice-cube buckets full of chilled champagne bottles on the Posh sites.'

Magenta teases. 'If I was one of those Artic migration birds I would turn around and elevate my Barnacle wing-foot to turbo-boost right back to where I came from.'

Pansy says. 'It's not funny!'

Magenta suggests. 'Sorry. I was just thinking out loud. The snow-geese are smart enough not to migrate here.'

Lars nags. 'I miss my Uncle Barnacle. I wouldn't want him singing or calling out to Pansy or myself when their homes are melting away. It would be a calamity for them to get washed up somewhere on a coastline caked-up in a sand dune or floating alongside popping-plastic nurdles.'

Piérre reports. 'Anushka and I were directed off course. We felt disorientated by the rising smog. We lost our singing voice. Our songs usually send messages to our flock, they give us the correct directions to migrate.'

Prof explains. 'The delicate seasonal clocks are distorted by the climate change. The interference messes with migration travel songs. Not being able to communicate is a problem. The climate disorder is to blame.'

Seagulls whinge. 'What about us? When we leave a place, we send echoes to our fellow seagulls. Huh! We haven't been echoing lately, have we?'

Cressida chomps. 'You gulls are too busy burying your stash of goodies!'

Kebab exclaims. 'Actually, today we went to the sandy beach and saw a little girl throw her carton of fizzy pop into the sea for fun. Chips swoops in and rescues the carton. Then, a naughty boy threw sand in Pizza's face for a joke!'

Perpetua tweets. 'I bet one of you slurped the fizzy pop first, scavenging for scraps!'

Pizza gawps. 'Rude!'

Prof blurts. 'It's true, the land, air, and ocean-animals get hurt and killed by mucky waters every single day. The plastic bags look like floating jellyfish to a turtle. MissRed and other sea creatures eat jellyfish as a staple diet.'

Ducky asks. 'Does that mean we are eating plastics?'

Prof replies. 'Micro-nurdles travel so fast they clog up the 'food chain' the ocean life feeds on.'

Ducky clucks. 'You can say that again!'

MissRed whinges. 'Plastic shrapnel stuffed in my mouth!'

Prof explains. 'MissRed, I am very sorry to say the humans have destroyed a third of the Earth's natural resources.'

Lars gasps. 'MissRed don't worry. It's not your fault. The humans caused it!'

MissRed moans. 'Ocean life sees humans as a huge threat to their existence. They live in fear that one day they may become extinct. Our natural food stock tastes horrible. Our young die before their time because they are not getting the nourishment they need to survive. The polar bears are threatened by the unexpected climate changes too. Not only the ice-melts disaster harms them but their hunting seasons are shortened by the continuous disturbance!'

Nelly sobs. 'The babies will have nowhere to play.'

MissRed sniffles. 'The ice melts into stepping ice blocks. The young treat it as a playground.'

Pansy agrees. 'I heard the playgrounds are fun.'

Ducky shouts. 'Not anymore!'

Professor MicroChip adds. 'To reduce, recycle and reuse sometimes is not an option for some. Billions of tonnes of waste are buried in humungous holes in the ground. That means enormous amounts of dangerous chemical gases escape into the atmosphere. Sewage and toxic chemicals escape into the sea. Oceans are no exception.'

Stag yawns. 'Have we finished yet? I am hungry!'

Blute reiterates. 'It could go on as far as one-hundred and fifty-years from now where some sea animals could become extinct. The young will not survive those ocean-fill wars. Do I make myself clear?'

Ducky bellows. 'Look at me, I stink of toxic gunk!'

MissRed adds. 'Look at oil-slick me!'

Stag whines. 'I had glass shrapnel cutting into my hooves!'

Froglips yells. 'I leapt on a sharp tin-pot lilypond!'

Masculus squeaks. 'I fled the enormous monster-cutter maniac!'

Nelly sobs. 'I broke my wings from a sticky plastic bag!'

Ed glares. 'It really isn't my fault.'

Scotty interjects. 'Aye wee laddie. We know it's not your fault.'

MissRed whinges. 'I want to go home now!'

Lars reassures. 'You will get home.'

Pansy meddles. 'Yes MissRed. You will be escorted by the most handsome dolphin pods.'

MissRed blushes. 'Ooh. Sounds lovely.'

Lars honks. 'Mm. Stop meddling Pansy!'

Pansy yawns. 'Blah-de-blah-de-blah. Lars, you can't even paddle properly.'

Bizzy urges. 'Leave him alone Pansy. Can't you see he has a twinkle in his eyes for MissRed.'

Bionca reminds. 'Ed? Are you listening?'

Ed replies. 'The more I listen with undivided attention, the more I learn. When I listen to nonsense babble, I get distracted. Yes, I am observing and taking notes in my head, for my school project.'

Professor MicroChip continues. 'Without water there would be no life on Earth. A high percentage is covered with water. A low percentage is fresh water. Humans can only drink a fraction of this fresh water. Most of the fresh water is not easy for them to reach as it is frozen in the glaciers and ice caps or buried underground.'

Blute retorts. 'I reckon the humans need to start economising on every drop of drinking water.'

Ed ponders. 'Does that mean, humans like me will be so desperate for drinking water that it could become more valuable than money or gold?'

Prof answers. 'It's a future issue. Your great-great-great-great grandchildren will bear the brunt of this polluted war. Do your research, Ed.'

Ed complains. 'I'm finding this topic confusing. I won't remember everything! My head is exploding and I am getting a bellyache.'

Prof adds. 'Could be, airborne mould and allergies from trees, weeds and grass.'

Blute moans. 'Anyone got any bright ideas!'

BirdCop wakes. 'Mm. Ask the bird scientist.'

Ed stutters. 'Erm. I think so.'

Prof smiles. 'Go ahead Ed, the platform is yours.'

Ed straightens his collar. 'Erm. Well. Our bamboozled climate needs a steady cooling system like a fridge-freezer that thinks for itself. Unlike our stupid fridge-freezers at home that break down, a lot. My grandad loves his rice-pudding medium to hot.'

Little Bro titters. 'Spit it out Bruv! What are you babbling about?'

Ed struggles. 'Er. Imagine a locomotive fridge-freezer full of frozen ice-cubes.'

Bionca gestures. 'Get to the point Ed?'

Ed splutters. 'My grandad eats a bowl of rice-pudding on a regular basis. Let's say he's stolen it from his best friend's breakfast table, which is set for three people.'

Little Bro quizzes. 'Whose breakfast table? Your grandad is a rice-pudding thief?'

Ed exhales. 'Let me speak out, Bruv! It doesn't have to be anyone's breakfast! It could be a boiled egg with buttery toasty soldiers. It's just a story, Bruv!'

Little Bro sniggers. 'Your grandad eats human soldiers for breakfast, Wow! You humans are weirdos.'

Ed snaps. 'It's a couple of slices of bread, toasted in an electric toaster. It scorches to a crusty golden-brown. We cut it into small shapes; we call them soldiers.'

Little Bro grins. 'Hahaha. Just winding you up. Got you Bruv!'

Ed resumes. 'Grandad robs a bowl of rice-pudding.'

Bionca points. 'You missed out the boiled egg, Ed?'

Ed exhales. 'Gosh! It's a runny egg yolk, not boiled. Grandad says the rice-pudding tastes better when it's not cold and not too hot. Grandad prefers the rice-pudding at the correct cooling point for him. So, you see, one day we may need that cooling system so all organisms can survive from the extreme temperatures.'

Little Bro mutters. 'What are you jabbering about Ed?'

Ed shushes. 'My theory is: grandad exhales a whistle blowing technique into his bowl of rice-pudding to cool it down. So, if the humans can bring the atmosphere down to a reasonable cooling point, it could work. Obviously, it would take a genius scientist to invent that mega machine.'

Blute chatters. 'Did somebody mention, "genius scientist?"'

BirdCop replies. 'Snoozing again, Blute?'

Ed asserts. 'Also, recycle, reuse and reduce a lot, and a lot more! More air-filled toxic pollution equals global boiling. Earth could end up a wrecking ball of fire!'

Ed affirms. 'Reducing by creating assorted flavoured edible seaweed packaging.'

MissRed intervenes. 'Oh! Help yourselves to our precious seaweed blankets, why don't you?'

Ed proclaims. 'No! No! No!'

MissRed reacts. 'Yes, Yes, Yes, Ed! You are just as bad!'

Greg explains. 'With assorted edible seaweed food packaging, it could reduce the need to throw away so many wrappers.'

Ed continues. 'The packaging can be eaten. It can also be recycled into a biodegradable compost. No chemicals are needed to produce it.'

Seagulls mutter. 'Ooh. Mm. Let's go beak-blitzing. Did Ed say, assorted edible flavoured packaging?'

Ed replies. 'Oh! Yes. I would choose a liquorish wrapper. You gulls could choose whatever you like. Your chores will be a delicious feast at the same time. You wouldn't get hash tagged "flying rat-bats."'

Seagulls remark. 'Rude!'

Cressida chatters. 'We like our cream poured from the upper milk-bottle parts. Especially, the dazzling assorted silver-coloured tops. Hm. You can't make that edible.'

Ed states. 'Aaah. A glass bottle takes one million years to decompose. Then again, it's not your fault you choose milk bottle cream. You will find it hard to peck edible carton lids.'

Perpetua says. 'Well. I suppose we could keep on slurping cream.'

MissRed hollers. 'I apologise for my outburst. The ocean-fills are transforming into huge areas of circling water, known as, 'gyres' and you can't make those edible. I was mistaken for a garbage patch!'

Prof interjects. 'There could be as much as five main garbage patches in the world. The Great Pacific garbage patch is the largest of them all. The huge cruise liners and other large water fleets drop trillions of tiny pieces of plastic and sharp metal fragments. These travel the seas and cluster into invisible rock-type dangerous sea-life destroying weaponries.'

MissRed sobs. 'Oh! No! The humans are using weapons now!'

Lars reassures. 'The garbage patches feel like weapons. Remember, the avalanches attacked you.'

MissRed sniffles. 'Yes, I understand now.'

Pansy tuts. 'Mm. Lars you are definitely in love with MissRed.'

MissRed blushes. 'Thank you. If there was such thing as a delightful goose, it has to be you.'

ED THE GUILTY SUPER-DUPER POLLUTER!

Ed confesses. 'I don't go on many overseas holidays, but I do remember going on a special holiday with my grandad and family members. It was a holiday of a lifetime. My grandad works really hard. I needed childcare, and the holiday was expensive. Driving is important to us. That vacation taught me to love nature. We visited beautiful places: mountains, forests, diving in the coral seas. We said that was the best holiday ever. When we went on skiing trips we took the ski train.'

Little Bro sighs. 'Ed? You, sure do need childcare.'

MissRed intrudes. 'Ed Williams! You are guilty! You have slithered over my scaly bald-head during your water-skiing jolly boat trips!'

Little Bro interjects. 'No! MissRed, you are wrong! Ed had a once-in-a-lifetime holiday. I give him a not-guilty verdict.'

Echoes of chitter-chatter erupts.

Professor MicroChip oversees. 'Ed is not guilty on this occasion. There are people who lavish on several overseas holidays each year. Ed is not one of those super polluters.'

Ed mumbles. 'I have friends who have loads and loads of air-flying luxury holidays on land and huge cruise liners. They are guilty not me!'

MissRed squeals. 'Huh! My verdict is still guilty! He's nothing but a little spoilt brat!'

Stag interjects. 'Sorry to change the boring subject. Does anyone miss the howling winds and snowstorms or wintry blizzards? I don't mind the soft flakes on my tongue. But today I felt a lot of pain in my hooves. I was trapped for ages because of the scruffy humans on their staycation. No hard feelings, Ed. It's still a guilty verdict from me.'

Robby adds. 'We like to play in the snowstorms.'

Nay wriggles. 'Yeah. I love the snow flurries tickling my ears and shuffling off my fluffy tail.'

Robby laughs. 'Yes Nay. You would prefer that instead of being stuck in a mucky plastic bag full of sharp cutlery. Erm. Sorry. Ed gets a guilty verdict from me.'

BirdCop grizzles. 'My feathers are itching for a guilty verdict!'

Little Bro shouts. 'You can't blame him. He's not a super polluter!'

Ed says. 'I am not guilty! You can't make me say I am guilty!'

Crowlip squawks. 'My rolling tongue likes the wintry frosty sugary petals. Mm. Perching on them beehives for the honeycomb crumbs. I like Ed and I know he's not a selfish brat. He gets a not guilty verdict from me.'

Cressida reveals. 'I like the snowy seasons when there's plenty of frozen sugary icicle buds and delicious thick flakes. The best thing is not being able to see Perpetua in the snowstorm. Anyway, Ed gets a not guilty verdict from us.'

Perpetua gripes. 'Rude!'

Citrus cackles. 'Boy? What do you peck at birthday parties? — If, you ever get invites.'

Little Bro interferes. 'You can't ask that question!'

BirdCop moots. 'Oh. Yes. We can!'

Ed beams. 'Now you're talking. Junk food takeaways. Der. Who cares whether it's healthy or not. Birthday celebrations and visits to the cinemas, theme parks with loads of delicious chicken nuggets and French fries, hotdogs and pizza and much more to choose from is an excuse to stuff my face and have fun. Before you ask, they do come in wrappers. Some parents aren't tyrants. If a kid at school has a birthday party, then everyone's invited. Huh! Even, the notorious yapping Nitty Nora gets an invite. You'd be an idiot if you turned down those invites. Who does that?'

Emee nips. 'Is your yapping Nitty Nora, a woof?'

Ed mutters. 'Nitty Nora doesn't woof, she yaps.'

Little Bro asks. 'Are you sure you don't fancy her?'

Ed shrugs. 'Bruv! You have got to be kidding!'

Pansy interrupts. 'Free-range! Organic! Do you kids recycle the packaging?'

Ed drools. 'Oh! No! We don't care if the birds or pigs are organic or not. And everyone leaves rubbish around. Der. It's a birthday celebration not a chore. The only thing on our minds is having plenty of fun!'

Digby heckles. 'Oh! Not again! Sausage rolls, pork pies and scotch egg sandwich buffets. I'm definitely giving that Ed a guilty verdict!'

Jax objects. 'My piggy ears will not listen to this greedy boy! Nothing more to be said. Other than, the boy is guilty!'

Crowlip mimics. 'You just told everyone that you are a super-polluting, messy meat-eating maniac! Why, didn't you say: "Cheese-and-pickle-sandwiches?" You don't have to mention the ham. Doofus!'

Little Bro splutters. 'Mm. You've just hung yourself Bruv.'

Ed cups his face. 'Oh! No! I'm guilty, aren't I?'

Little Bro replies. 'Twit! You've just slam-dunked yourself, face down in a puddle of magpie turbo-poops.'

Emee woofs. 'Doofus boy!'

Ed responds. 'What! Emee, I can hear you crystal-clear now!'

Emee barks. 'Lunk!'

Ed chuckles. 'Are you calling me names, Emee?'

Emee yaps. 'Yes Ed. Idiot!'

Ed declares. 'Judge and jury, please let me explain. I told the truth. I didn't lie.'

Professor MicroChip answers. 'Go ahead Ed, we are all listening.'

Ed explains. 'My grandad drives a fully electric humming car. I take the bus to school. Other families need to travel long distances to work and drive their children to out-of-area schools. Everyone in our village goes shopping. Cars are important, is that a climate crime? Are we guilty of living?'

Professor answers. 'Mm. What an unusual question Ed. School is important. Work is necessary. We all have to eat. If non-electrical vehicles were banned then taxis and coaches and trains would be heavily relied on. The fuel pollution wouldn't change. The expense is mammoth and money is sparse these days. There would be more and more round trips to school. In fact, I can't answer that question Ed. Let's not forget, socialising could be a thing of the past.'

The Prof continues. 'Children have holidays to teach them to love nature and visit beautiful places which, I hasten to add, totals carbon footprints. Witnessing mountains and waterfall features would be impossible in local communities. Gosh! I'm stunned for words. I really cannot answer that.'

Scotty comments. 'Aye, some children go to private schools. Aye. Privileged it may sound, but nobody can tell me that's a wrong instinct for a parent or guardian to want the best education for their children. Everybody ought to be taught to love nature.'

Prof comments. 'I cannot answer that question either.'

Ed rants. 'It's not fair! I'm not a rich posh boy! My grandad doesn't own holiday homes all over the world. I have one Xbox console and one mobile phone. The posh lot have loads of money to spend. They can buy anything they want and don't know what chores are! Stop ganging-up on me!'

Prof decides. 'Ed, sit down and write an unusual letter. Just think of the future unborn. Try to imagine Earth is full of airborne pollution. What kind of world are they living in?'

Little Bro nudges. 'Write that weird message, Bruv.'

Scotty adds. 'Aye, Ed wee laddie, give it your best script. Remember you are the unborn.'

Ed thinks. 'Mm. How can I possibly have unborn great, great, great, great grandchildren? I have never had a girlfriend. In fact, I have never been blown a kiss.'

Bionca bleats. 'Ed, just do it!'

Ed swipes nuts. 'Phew! I'll plonk myself in a quiet space by that old chestnut tree to think about what I am going to write. What am I supposed to say? Ouch!'

Crowlip tweets. 'Can't wait to hear this one.'

Ed scrambles for his pen and paper.

Professor MicroChip smiles. 'Ed think of it as your school project.'

Ed begins to feel hazy; he gazes to the sky.

Little Bro snoops. Ed rubs his head until his spectacles fall from his face into a pool of chestnuts. Little Bro keels over in fits of laughter. Ed slumps and wriggles. He gets twitchy until he finds himself mumbling in a dream-state.'

Emee sniffs. 'Ed? Are you zonked-out dead? You've been slumped down here for a while.'

Crowlip tweets. 'He's snoozing for his school project.'

Little Bro ushers. 'Shoo! You two.'

Suddenly, Ed startles himself by jolting out of his snooze. Immediately he pens the unborn poetic message until his assignment is complete.

Ed calls out. 'Finished!'

ED'S UNBORN MESSAGE

Professor MicroChip greets. 'Ed, take a deep breath, sip a cool drink, then recite.'

Ed opens the scrunchy pages from his scraggy school jotter.

Bionca urges. 'Come on Ed, we are waiting.'

Bizzy echoes. 'Ooh. Ed looks serious.'

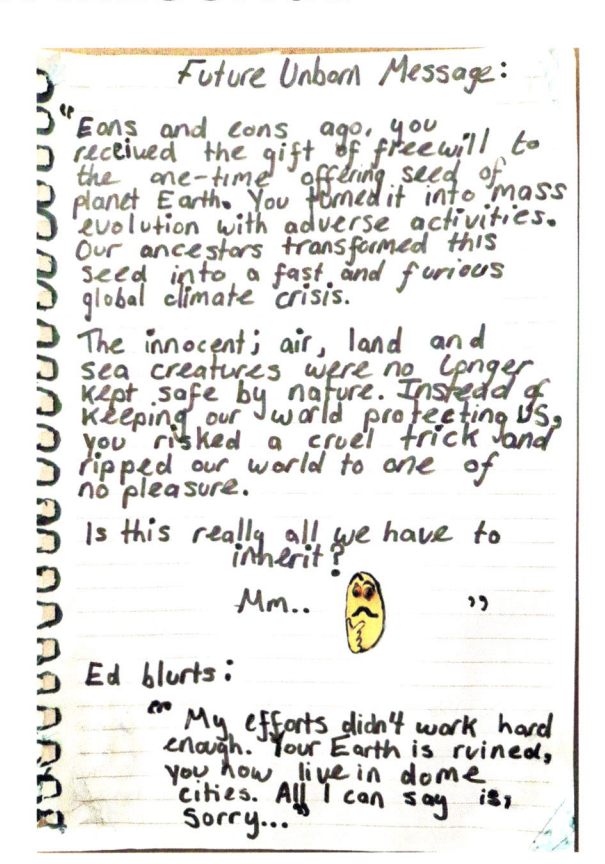

Future Unborn Message:

"Eons and eons ago, you received the gift of freewill to the one-time offering seed of planet Earth. You turned it into mass evolution with adverse activities. Our ancestors transformed this seed into a fast and furious global climate crisis.

The innocent; air, land and sea creatures were no longer kept safe by nature. Instead of keeping our world protecting us, you risked a cruel trick and ripped our world to one of no pleasure.

Is this really all we have to inherit?

Mm.. "

Ed blurts:

" My efforts didn't work hard enough. Your Earth is ruined, you now live in dome cities. All I can say is, sorry..."

Little Bro asks. 'You and your wobbly butt were having a jolly old natter under the old chestnut tree. Who was you talking to?'

Ed answers. 'Mm. Not sure. Let me think.'

Little Bro prods. 'Tell me Bruv?'

Ed tickles his chin. 'Erm. I think it may have been my, great-great-great-great grandson. He lives in a huge dome; he calls it home.'

Little Bro says. 'I haven't the foggiest idea what you're talking about, Bruv.'

Ed explains. 'Well, with all the babbling of what we humans should or ought to do, I may have met my future unborn. He said the sky isn't real, the world has makeshift artificial ceilings in Dome Cities. The fresh countryside doesn't exist. They have wildlife and birds flying around nestling in their own natural spaces we created for them.'

Blute tweets. 'They really have birds and no fresh air?'

BirdCop chatters. 'Nothing new then.'

Rocky bleats. 'No juicy curly whirly worms to dig up?'

Ed replies. 'I didn't ask.'

Professor MicroChip exhales. 'I perish the thought of humans living in domes.'

Ed says. 'I asked him if he likes living in a dome.'

Bizzy quizzes. 'What did he say?'

Ed retorts. 'He said, this is our world. We know about Noah and the Ark and other cultures from the past. Your historians left scriptures that our historians find amusing.'

Prof probes. 'What do you think he meant by "amusing?"'

Ed replies. 'Survival is the issue. Their ancestors made an effort to bash planet Earth into a wrecking ball.'

Bionca interrupts. 'Anything else Ed?'

Ed replies. 'Yes. They have one thing in common.'

Little Bro intrudes. 'What?'

Ed recalls. "They need food to survive just like us. Everything is dome-organic fresh produce. The importance of having somewhere to live and feel safe and secure. They relate and unite with all cultures; they prefer the feeling of love and belonging rather than squabbling. He said, leisure is hard to explain, but they like the football stories."

Little Bro probes. 'Is that it?'

Ed closes. 'Bruv, I heard him echo: "Nice football boots." Then I woke up with a sore bobbly butt-cheek.'

Little Bro assumes. 'Oh, Bruv. Without a doubt, I reckon you met your future self.'

Emee sniggers. 'It's a good job you woke up. Otherwise, the unborn might have given you a knuckle-sandwich on the nose! And, maybe you met the future yapping woof-woof Nitty Nora again!'

Ed answers. 'Well. He looks just like me in my dream today. Kar-azee awesome!'

Professor MicroChip taps. 'There's no Kar-azee awesome about that, lad. Imagine outdoor activity will go down in their history as a myth. Because, the solar radiation and humidity on the human body needs a cooling system to regulate the temperature. Dome Cities will be homes for the unborn unless a miracle is engineered or a new planet evolves.'

Ed shades his eyes. 'Gosh! Artificial to us will be real to them.'

Little Bro backtracks. 'Remember that rice-pudding theory?'

Ed shrugs. 'Oh! Bruv, let's not revisit there again.'

MissRed shuffles. 'I think I'll need to give my shell a good ruffle before I start! Maybe, sealife will live in makeshift sea-domes. Huh. And, fed on rice-pudding and assorted jelly fish plastic bags!'

Little Bro assures. 'Not in your lifetime, MissRed.'

MissRed nitpicks. 'Oh. What balderdash! I, suppose my unborn will not be born at all. We can't live in domes. Our unborn will be living off microplastic nurdles! I don't like jelly fish and no one can make me eat those wobbly bobbly stingy things. See you later at the secret garden. Enjoy your weirdo talks!'

Ed replies. 'Eavesdropping is not good for you, MissRed.'

Little Bro and Ed lag behind. They decide to take a peek at The Recyclosaurus.

Little Bro cheers. 'Ed, I'm going to give you an unforgettable adventure. Come on. Stop dawdling.'

Ed enquires. 'What's going on?'

Little Bro urges. 'Look, you said you wanted an adventure.'

Ed says. 'Mm. Well in that case. I'll follow your lead.'

Little Bro chuckles. 'The one and only; Recyclosaurus!'

Ed guesses. 'It looks like a lock-tight, top-secret mechanical monster.'

Little Bro confirms. 'Tutt, tutt. The Recyclosaurus is no secret to me. Der. I'm an EggBanger!'

Little Bro instructs. 'Let's creep to that oak tree, pretend you're a mountain climber, ferret through the leaves and clamber across the thick stumps. Then grapple with that joint-like thick stem as near to The Recyclosaurus' scaley neck. I'll grab that thick jointed rod-like bendy branch. You are going to have an unforgettable joy ride.'

Ed dodges. 'Ouch!'

Little Bro meddles. 'Come on! Swing like Tarzan! Thrash your way through the scratchy leaves. Oh. Accept the leaf-slaps in the face when you least expect it.'

The branches whip Ed's butt-cheeks until he gets shockwaves. Another leafy branch smacks him in the face a few times, feeling like a few wasp stings.

Ed freaks. 'I can't do this! I am not a climber! I can't lose my specs in that dumpster bucket! I'm getting shockwaves in my butt-cheeks. Now, I have rips in my trouser pants.'

Little Bro giggles. 'This is what you call an adventure. Stop behaving like a coward. Get a grip Ed!'

Ed chuffs. 'Well, if you put it like that, I suppose I could put up with a few more branch-butt lashes. Ouch!'

Suddenly, The Recyclosaurus rears its front hind legs, thumps its feet and mounts its front arms, still clutching filthy rubbish buckets. The branches start tweaking, swaying backwards and forwards behaving totally out-of-control.

Ed shouts. 'Whoa! Steady on you wild thing!'

Little Bro splutters. 'Oh! No!'

Ed chants. 'We're catapulting into that slop bucket on The Recyclosaurus' claw!'

Out of the blue, The Recyclosaurus' tail twitches and rustles. It guffaws to see Ed and Little Bro ferret inside the rancid buckets.

The Recyclosaurus raises its left arm three times; it makes three hi-fives, a salute and spit.

Ed blurts. 'Gosh! It's moving!'

Little Bro yells. 'Blah! It's spitting!'

Ed blinkers. 'Wow! Wee! Kar-razee Awesome!'

Little Bro and Ed scramble to ground level.

Ed wipes his sweaty head. 'I'm having the best day of my life.'

Little Bro suggests. 'Let's give the Bird Walk contest a miss. Wait and see what I've got planned for us next.'

A CAULDRON SPELL FOR NITTY NORA

Little Bro utters. 'I'm glad you're having a great adventure.'
Ed replies. 'You've made all this happen for me today.'
Little Bro smirks. 'Mm. It could have been worse.'
Ed remarks. 'What do you mean?'
Little Bro jokes. 'Well. You could have met a Yeti big-foot behind the bushes this morning. Besides, you'll forget about me after today. Once school is re-open, you'll be having fun with your mates.'
Ed mopes. 'Most days I avoid the notorious yapping Nitty Nora.'
Little Bro probes. 'Is she your girlfriend?'
Ed grouches. 'Nitty Nora is no girlfriend of mine. I try to stay out of her way.'
Emee kangaroo jumps and circles around. 'Nitty Nora is a yapping woof girl.'
Ed affirms. 'Huh. Nitty Nora bullies me at school whenever she gets the chance. She baits, teases, mocks and taunts me.'
Little Bro ushers Ed towards Professor MicroChip's forbidden, 'DO NOT ENTER, magic workshop.'

Little Bro escorts. 'Look! This is a Wizards Caudron. That Nitty Nora woof girl won't be bullying you again!'

Little Bro flickers. 'These pages are forbidden.'

Ed fusses. 'In that case, I think we should go now.'

Little Bro whispers. 'It's okay, so long as we are discreet and silent as a mouse.'

Ed chortles. 'Not like that little gobby mouse, Masculus.'

Little Bro improvises. 'Bruv. That yapping Nora will be in alot of bother with this spell.'

Ed murmurs. 'Bring it on!'

Little Bro cheers. 'Follow my lead, my wizard apprentice. Take this yew-tree branch. Wave it around like a magic wand anti-clockwise, three times only. It has a fearsome powerful strength. Take your courage my fearless Robin Hood. Now, mix the spell into a brew to show-and-tell.'

Ed conjures a spell for Nitty Nora:

"With this wand, open wizardry protection spell for me, Ed Williams,
If, Nitty Nora bullies me or tells lies,
Cauldron spell will set the smelly maggots into wild-flies,
Rise from ponds, streams and rivers they doth pop,
Cook the picnic brew of parasite slops,
Once, twice or thrice,

Pack the floating bugs lock-tight,
Scratch your skull until it itches,
Your head doth twirl, whirl and twitches,
Nitty Nora watches the clock go tick-tock,
Glitter lice sprinkles, give her head a big shock!!"

A R Trent

Little Bro cackles. 'Huh. No need for any fisty cuffs. Nitty Nora won't be bothering you again.'

Ed interjects. 'Bruv! I don't bash girls. As a matter of fact, I don't get my fisty cuffs out for anyone. As you know, I am a wimpy looking scrawny kid. The only boxing I know, is Xbox gaming.'

THE BIRD WALK PAGEANT

Wow! The bird walk pageant is taking place today. Blute announces. 'BirdCop and I, will be ranking competitors for cleanliness, virtue and honesty.'

BirdCop makes a full inspection and gives a quick news flash:

'Ozzy, our dedicated ecowarrior garden sparrow, was looking forward to taking the prize-winning trophy today. Unfortunately, he flew into a sturdy wooden shed roof, speeding over-the-limit and met his nemesis by making a hard thud like a ton of bricks on a concrete garden path, head-first. He died on the spot with his bill gaped open still dangling his catch of the day. A yummy juicy curly whirly worm. I'm sorry to say he won't be taking part in the pageantry today or any other day. He's in Bird Heaven, rest his soul. The silly fool is still disqualified.'

Blute notes. 'As a matter of fact, Max, you're disqualified too, for not working as a team with Ozzy. Rumour has it, a man was hanging his washing out on the line and had a huge fright.'

Citrus mutters. 'Mm. Huh! Idiot! He nearly caught the early dawning cock-a-doodle-doo morning worm. Ozzy buckeroos into a shed and bucks his head and he's dead. Bird heaven rest his soul.'

Ducky clucks. 'I'm not in a very good mood either. Those rusty love-locks have given me too many clonks on the head today. Someone else can take my trophy! I quit!'

BirdCop intervenes. 'Your insolence and non-virtuous manner automatically gives you a disqualification. You indeed, have a bad attitude!'

Masculus squeaks. 'What about me? I'm virtuous and smart. I can strum a melodic one-mouse-band symphony on my violin, unlike the buffoons here.'

Ducky quacks. 'Who are you calling a buffoon? Huh! Go and jump into a custard tart with your pile of sawdust!'

BirdCop interjects. 'As you are aware, the winner will be judged mostly on virtue. Which means honourability to each other. Do we understand? Move your butts off my platform!'

BirdCop notices. 'What have we here? Fish, Chips, Pizza, Kebab and Hotdog. Have you been to the Posh sites today?'

The gulls freeze stock-still. 'Er. Well. It was like this. We took the wrong turning and ended up at the deli posh sites.'

Chips chirps. 'We were good girls, weren't we gulls? Before you ask, of course, we cracked on with our chores.'

BirdCop looms. 'What have we here! Five bulging bellies! Mm. Loitering around the Posh sites again! You are all disqualified! You are not worthy or virtuous you gluttony gulls! Get off my platform at once!'

Blute summons. 'Magpies! Your dribbling beaks has been siphoning milk-bottle-top cream again! No criminals allowed. Shove off!'

BirdCop beckons. 'Crowlip, your scruffy hooter is dripping green-snot. You are one-hundred-percent, disqualified!'

Blute gestures. 'Our two peace doves will show you what a pageant is about.'

Annie squawks. 'Stop pushing me!'

Polly squeals. 'No! You're pushing me! Ouch!'

Annie chants. 'Stop fibbing!'

Blute shouts. 'Call yourselves, peace-loving doves? Tootle off my stage!'

BirdCop calls. 'Next please!'

Lars honks. 'Aww! The green lasso is in knots. We will tumble off this stage! How could we let this happen?'

Pansy strops. 'Argh! Silly, finnicky pernickety pink and green ropes!'
BirdCop guffaws. 'Give me strength you foolish geese! Shuffle off!'
Blute exhales. 'Next!'

Citrus cackles. 'I am dishonest. I am not virtuous. In fact, I am a self-confessed gambler. I saw a one-foot racing pigeon drop down stone dead. He threw himself by cart-wheeling into a wind turbine. He was carrying my winning betting slip. I disqualify myself. Mm. Huh!'

BirdCop replies. 'It fills me with happiness to accept your disqualification. May I suggest you contact the Bird Gamblers Anonymous Group, before you leave LA-LA Forest Park!'

Citrus answers. 'Mm. Huh. I will do that today.'

Anushka and Piérre wave. 'We got lost because we couldn't sing our migration song, so we don't trust ourselves to flutter in a straight line on a pageant stage. We disqualify ourselves.'

BirdCop cups her face in despair. 'Point taken, now get off!'

Rocky broods. 'I saw Ozzy fall to his death, still clinging to his catch of the day. That juicy curly whirly worm sure got away. I am not an honest birdy.'

BirdCop shouts. 'You get an instant disqualification for being a story-telling gibberish fibber!'

Blute sighs. 'Anyone else!'

Magenta flaps. 'I prance and strut my dainty bird-tapping claws. My dress has adorning sparkling sequences. I twist and twirl like a whipping-top carousel. I pirouette showing full plumage. I sway and swirl my cerise handbag around my nifty neck. I curtsy and serenade you pouting heart kisses.'

BirdCop claps. 'Bravo! At last!'

Blute cheers. 'What an exquisite performer. More!!'

Nelly utters. 'My tippy-toe claws can't dance today and my feathers are broken I won't squint or squirm, my tears are dry. I am doing the drill and getting a thrill.'

BirdCop tweets. 'You are a mild-hearted canary. You kept your stage fright intact, after notorious Nasty Patsy's attack.'

Blute applauds. 'First Prize and the trophy goes to the amazing Magenta all the way from Jamaica. You are virtuous. It must be difficult trying to keep old Citrus under control. Make sure he attends the BGAG meeting today.'

BirdCop announces. 'Runner-up shield goes to the one and only Nelly canary.'

BENEATH THE OASIS

Little Bro decides. 'Ed, you're ready for the next adventure beneath the oasis.'

Skipper and Scamp await the whooshing Springusaurus water slide.

Scamp bellows. 'Have a good time beneath the oasis!'

Ed squints. 'Huh! What, oasis?'

Little Bro teases. 'Exploring the water adventures.'

Ed mocks. 'Yeah. Exploring rip currents beneath the oasis. Or, the pair of us getting washed up on that grubby Bird BootCamp.'

Little Bro larks. 'You won't see any tidal waves where we are heading. But don't touch the marine life or the coral reefs – or else!'

Professor MicroChip arrives. 'I thought you might need a basic tutorial on what you should be wearing for your next adventure. Snorkelling underwater can be a hazard. Firstly, here's your full-face snorkel mask. It's a snug fit with a good seal. The anti-fog spray is useful, so we'll give it a little spray in the right places. Here's your snorkel pipe to put around your mouth. There's a drain valve just in case you get a leak.'

Ed exhales. 'What leak? Oh. No! I am going to drown today in that leaky mask. I'll never get home!'

The EggBangers eavesdrop.

Grandma EggBanger reassures. 'There is no chance of you drowning today young man. We are fully experienced guides; we will protect you. Do you understand?'

Ed inhales. 'Erm. I think so.'

Emee and Crowlip moan. 'What about us?'

Professor MicroChip explains. 'No doggy paddling allowed. And I have never seen a snorkelling crow.'

Crowlip squawks. 'Okay, see you later. I'm off to the secret garden to get some grub! Maybe, we could meet you at the other eatery?'

Emee mocks. 'Yeah. We'll catch up with you later. Wherever you are.'

Professor MicroChip continues: 'Ed, you'll need perfect-fit snorkel fins to put on your bare feet and a diving wet-suit. Sunblock is necessary because you'll still be getting exposure to the sun. Wear this rash guard because it will protect your skin from abrasions or rashes in the waters. Let's call it double-protection.'

Bizzy prods. 'Are you listening Ed?'

Ed gibbers. 'Err. Think so.'

Greg coaches. 'Let's get ready. Put masks on, head-peak, attach snorkel pipe and start practising breathing. Slip fins on and walk backwards in the water. Don't worry about your oxygen levels because everything is sorted.'

Little Bro mocks. 'No blubbering Ed. When we complete this adventure, how do you fancy rocketing up the Springusaurus' flying ramp above the waterfall slide into the air?'

Ed teases. 'Hahaha, you'll end up getting a good clonking on your egg head.'

Bionca interjects. 'Rude!'

Bizzy adds. 'Double -rude!'

Scotty advises. 'Now, wee laddie, put your face down gently into the water surface and look down. Breathe easy, in and out.'

Ed pops up. 'Wow! Kar-azee! Awesome! I can do it!'

Greg instructs. 'Now, swim around, head down on the top and take little peeps down under.'

Big Bro advises. 'Start kicking with your fins. Your feet will be secure and comfortable enough to flipper them around. No doggy paddling allowed. Make sure that your hands are behind your back and kick forward. Kick above the water for now. You can use your hands for dog paddling when you get back later.'

Ed asks. 'I may be safe now but what about later?'

Bizzy says. 'Take this whistle and diving red-and-white flag.'

Ed replies. 'The flag might come in handy.'

Big Bro assures. 'You won't need it.'

Bionca beckons. 'Come on! Let's take a dive before snorkelling beneath the oasis. Hold your breath, roll forward, feet up and above the water because it acts as a weight to push you down. Your nose will feel funny at first. The pressure on your ears will pop if you pinch or blow your nose. Do you read me, Ed?'

Ed makes a thumbs up. 'Yes.'

Bizzy spots a sleeping parrotfish under a coral-reef ledge. 'Ed! Look! Its body is cocooned in a slimy bubble it has just blown around itself. They usually do this when it is dark to hide from predators.'

Ed winces. 'Are we predators?'

Big Bro replies. 'No, we are not predators. The sleeping parrotfish hides its smell from others to protect itself.'

Ed utters. 'Aah, I get it.'

Greg adds. 'You're on to a winner with your school project, Ed.'

Prof points. 'Peek at those flamenco dancing snails.'

Greg nudges. 'See the loose coral reef and snail dancers paraded in sync around them.'

Big Bro chants. 'Prize-winning Spanish dancers under the oasis pageant! Hooray! Hooray! Hooray!'

Scotty follows. 'Aye! Aye! Aye! Bravo!'

Ed signals. 'Awesome!'

Prof examines. 'Let me check my depth gauge. Hm. I would say eighteen-to-twenty-metres.'

Ed gawks. 'What are those funny looking fish?'

Grandma replies. 'I'll answer your question before I leave. Firstly, these are colourful clown fish circling us. But at the moment they are not protecting themselves by covering up with the usual slimy mucus that acts as an armour against stings. We wear our wetsuits and they cluster up to the anemone's stinging tentacles. In return, the clown fish keep the sea anemone clean.'

Ed shrieks. 'Ugh! I don't like the look of those sea anemones. They look like wriggling worms growing from the seabed.'

Grandma says. 'You could say they both work in partnership.'

Ed ponders. 'Mm. I could use this as research for my school project? Erm. Swirling crystalising underwater knotty spaghetti worms. Err. Broccoli algae tents. An oasis forest full of synchronised silhouette ballet dancers.'

Little Bro prods. 'Can I help you? You seem lost in thought Bruv.'

Ed responds. 'Yeah. Just brainstorming, deep in school-assignment thoughts.'

Greg teases. 'Clown boy!'

Ed questions. 'What is a coral reef?'

Big Bro explains. 'A coral reef is made up from tiny animals, called polyps. These polyps can be hard as rocks on the outside. Then the reef will build itself into a coral polyp.'

Bionca clarifies. 'Yeah! It'll attach itself to a rock on the sea floor. The single coral will multiply itself in half and build another coral; and so on.'

Professor MicroChip elaborates. 'On a wide scale when billions of corals join together, it's known as a huge single coral colony. That's what makes a coral reef the greatest, like the Great Barrier Reef.'

Ed gasps. 'Epic!'

Scotty points to the manta rays. 'Look at the manta rays. They are just visiting to take a well-earned scrub down.'

Ed signals. 'What do you mean?'

Scotty answers. 'All these little glistening rainbow fishes and coral algae are living organisms. This is their cleaning stations. They get nibbled at, including their mouths and gills.'

Ed gurgles. 'Ugh! Blah!'

Greg says. 'Look at it this way: the little parasites and the teeny, weeny nibbling fishes get fed and the manta's get a good coral reef scrub-a-dub. It's a win-win for both.'

Ed jolts. 'Ouch! That sticky out coral reef nearly gave me a buckeroo on the butt-cheeks!'

Scotty chuckles. 'Nae. Wee, laddie. It missed you.'

Ed fusses. 'I'm wearing a good protective butt-cheek wetsuit, aren't I?'

Bizzy points. 'Look at those cuttlefish hiding behind that rocky reef. They are waiting for their baby cuttlefish to hatch in two months' time.'

Ed flabbergasts. 'Wow! They look like Christmas baubles hanging from underneath a coral ceiling.'

Bionca interjects. 'They'll need lots of worms, crabs any fishes that lay on the corals for their young. They like a good feast.'

Bizzy adds. 'They can camouflage themselves from enemies too and can easily hide their eggs.'

Greg remarks. 'Plankton, is the term used for the feed.'

Ed replies. 'Mm. What a useful piece of information for a written project.'

Greg points to the Plan B produce. 'There is an abundance of tough seaweed grass here.'

Scotty waves. 'Aye, Greg! Tell them about the bag poem. Down here, right now.'

Ed cheers. 'Yeah!'

Greg recites:
"There's a never-ending stash from down under the oasis trash,
Hidden under the camouflage Spotted Wobbegong Shark,
Purest dark olive green toughest seaweed grass,
It's chemical free and compostable soil,
Virtually no emissions, needs no permission,
Cheers from down under bubble and gargle with glee,
LA-LA Forest Park's Plan B, free carrier bag for life."

*<div align="right">**A R Trent**</div>*

Professor MicroChip reminds. 'I think Ed is ready for the next adventure.'

Little Bro chuckles. 'Brace yourself Ed, your next voyage awaits you.'

Ed remarks. 'Gosh! You EggBangers know how to have fun.'

Little Bro affirms. 'We have inbuilt microphones. We can hear each other too.'

Ed rubs his forehead. 'Now you tell me!'

OCEAN CRYSTAL CAVES

Professor MicroChip summons the EggBangers. Their timeless travelling vessel awaits to take them to the caves to encounter more of the undersea life.

Little Bro urges. 'Come on Bruv, no peeping.'

Ed snoops. 'Woo! Whoa! Am I imagining?'

Professor MicroChip explains. 'No. You are now witnessing some of the rarest sea creatures under the oasis.'

Ed crouches. 'Will they bite me?'

Greg replies. 'No. If, we took the tropical tour maybe a bite would be in store for you.'

Bionca laughs. 'Greg is teasing you.'

Ed spots Wobbegong sharks. 'Who are they hiding from?'

Bizzy says. 'They hide from predators by camouflaging in a blanket of seaweed. They look flat and can master themselves to disguise.'

Ed reacts. 'Good stuff.'

Professor MicroChip adds. 'Orectolobus maculatus' is another name for them. It's true that they can blend in easily under the sea.'

Big Bro adds. 'Look at them! They are the coolest chilled out sharks, their whiskers are so relaxed. This one is around, ten-point-five-feet in size and has light and dark markings. But I think the triangle between their eyes is weird.'

Scotty says. 'Aye, they come to life at night and gobble up the tiny fishes. They have been known in other parts of the world to eat large marine creatures.'

Ed blinks. 'Don't let MissRed hear you say that.'

Greg says. 'They can be seen in the Indian Ocean, South China Sea, even the Japanese coasts. They prefer warm tropical waters, as far as I am aware.'

Ed gasps. 'Wicked!'

Big Bro remarks. 'Look! There's a family of Longnose Sucker Butterfly fish.'

Ed inhales. 'Epic!'

Big Bro chortles. 'This will be brilliant, for your research project.'

Ed gargles. 'Argh! I'm glad that Longnose fish subject is over.'

Big Bro teases. 'They are around nine-inches long but can grow bigger. They are peaceful and don't like aggression as a rule, so they won't nip you in the butt-cheeks. Hahaha.'

Ed flabbergasts. 'Glad to hear that Big Bro. I do like their bright-coloured yellow markings and black-and-white faces.'

Bizzy adds. 'They like to pick at the corals and have a preference for blood worms and algae, even land and animal matter.'

Ed gags. 'Argh!'

Bionca laughs. 'You have a long-pointy snout, just like that Longnose Sucker Butterfly fish.'

Ed twitches. 'No way!'

Bizzy cackles. 'Don't bother asking for a sick-bag.'

Ed glugs. 'Yippee! Let's move on.'

After vacating the secret ocean-liner vessel. They all snorkel to the surface.

Little Bro races. 'Ed? Beat you to the crystal caves. But we've got to hop over those floating giant stepping stones first.'

Ed gargles. 'Easy-peasy, lemony-squeezy!'

EggBangers bursts out laughing.

Ed bellows. 'This is not, a knockabout fun! I'm going to tip up-side-down!'

Little Bro howls. 'I must admit, they are not, your usual stepping stones!'

Ed pokes. 'Explain!'

Little Bro chortles. 'They are harmless emerging rock-size floating wobbling sea-slugs. If you step on them, it tickles, which makes them giggly. Wobbling sea-slugs always splash for fun.'

Ed gawps. 'Honestly Bruv! Do you need anything else on that waffle?'

Little Bro replies. 'Waffle? What do you mean?'

Ed answers. 'Us humans say: 'Shut up and, stop waffling! Right now, I am not feeling any bubbles of excitement. Except for pooping in my wetsuit!'

Greg reassures. 'Take your time Ed. We've nearly reached the shallow end to where we need to be.'

Bizzy laughs. 'Poor Ed, he's skidding over those floating sea-slugs.'

Bionca giggles. 'At least that's all he's skidding on.'

Professor MicroChip gives a scenario of the origins of crystal caves:

'The ocean caves are caused by erosion from waves. The caves get fractured and weak which gives them their shapes. Lots of minerals mix together and form into crystals of all varieties and qualities.'

Ed beams. 'Spectacular!'

Professor affirms. 'These are our secret crystal chambers. They are captivating geometric gems. You'll be getting a close-up view at these thrilling majestic sacred rocks. All crystals are gifts from natural resources from Planet Earth.'

Scotty ushers. 'This way folks.'

Ed expresses. 'Cool! Nice one! Insects and plants – they twinkle like rainbow garden lights. The crystals have razor-sharp diamond cuts.'

Professor MicroChip recaps. 'Insects and plants naturally glow and illuminate from the crystals. You could say they're another gift from the natural world.'

Greg ushers Ed. 'See that monument, it's my favourite. A colossal Smoky Quartz geode. It glows like the moon at night. It has a strong link with the Earth and is concerned about the environment.'

Ed wonders. 'So, it could pull in good energies from the universe to help the planet, in some way?'

Greg answers. 'Mm. Something like that.'

Ed points. 'Sweet, a diamond orange.'

Scotty blinks. 'Aye. Some say this crystal gives you luck. It's called, "Citrine."'

Ed remarks. 'So, it's like a lucky charm.'

Scotty chortles. 'Aye, Ed wee laddie, you could put it that way.'

Bizzy prods. 'Ed? Look at that 'Rose Quartz.' I love it so much. It has caring energies.'

Ed gestures. 'Mm. Maybe, Lars could've tucked a tiny pocket of the Rose Quartz shards under his pocket wings.'

Bionca jolts. 'Why?'

Ed replies. 'MissRed might have fallen in love with Lars.'

Bizzy sighs. 'All the crystals in the world could never get MissRed to fall in love with Lars.'

Bionca shouts. 'Gawk at that purple Amethyst geode! It's special to me. We all have our favourite little pocket crystals. I feel safe around this one.'

Ed blurts. 'I won't be needing one for Nitty Nora now. I'm sorted.'

Little Bro nudges. 'Shush!'

Big Bro chants. 'Green Fluorite! This geode is the best! It has a heal-yourself quality about it.'

Ed exclaims. 'Can it cure my stingy bottom that's been whipped by high thrashing branches?'

Big Bro quizzes. 'Have you been clambering up something, Ed?'

Little Bro pokes. 'Ed, I hope I'm not about to meet the world's biggest snitch.'

Ed huffs. 'Big Bro – seriously? I don't have climber's legs. As you know, I scream like a baby and act like a weak unadventurous wimpy kid.'

Little Bro calls. 'Watch me climb up that humungous geode Tiger's eye. Whoa! Come on! Let's get ready to scramble!'

Ed shrieks. 'I don't have climber's legs. I thought you would've worked that one out by now.'

Little Bro gets euphoric. 'Easy peasy! Let's just do it!'

Ed plunges. 'Okay! Whoa! Up the crystal mountain we clamber into the Tiger's eye, geode. Sweet! I feel on top of the world! Wey! Hey! Good stuff, Little Bro!'

Bizzy laughs. 'Ed, catch them colours! They're brown, yellow, pink, blue and red stripes.'

Professor MicroChip adds. 'These rocks and crystals let off energies. The Tiger's eye in particular has parallel fibre patterned stripes which makes it one of the unique ones.'

Ed asks. 'Why?'

Prof answers. 'It is deep and rich in friendship.'

Ed worries. 'My best friend is my grandad. He will be concerned about me. I mustn't get home too late.'

Scotty comforts Ed. 'In the Secret Garden, time is the essence which means there is no time, no hours, minutes, seconds including nanoseconds. A funday means just that. We can assure you Ed, just forget about the time factor.'

The EggBangers chant. 'Get ready for knockabout fun on the Springusaurus!'

THE SPRINGUSAURUS

Ed beams. 'Wicked! It takes a waterfall to the upper limit!'

Little Bro yells. 'You'll be hanging on its springy neck, having the time of your life. This Springusaurus has high flume rides spiralling downwards into the water. We can jump on and off our surfboard and slide partway. It will then turn into a whirlpool and splash us into the bottom pool for fun.'

Ed splutters. 'At least it doesn't have slop buckets.'

Skipper and Scamp scurry into the flowerbeds and flump themselves into a fresh puddle of tadpoles, minding their own business.

Skipper tips up. 'Oopsy. Sorry, we didn't mean to disturb you.'

Scamp retorts. 'I'm going to hunt for the fattiest, slimiest munchy-meat slugs. It's better than the gunge we've been eating lately.'

Skipper hollers. 'Yippee! We can stay up into the nocturnal hours then come back and have a little feast after we've had some fun all to ourselves.'

Scamp shuffles. 'I want a go on the Springusaurus too. I need a refreshing spring-cleaning!'

Skipper puffs. 'Jax needs a pig-butt shove. He's hogging the queue.'
Jax snorts. 'Hm. What a load of ill-mannered hogwash.'

Digby strops: 'Hear this!'

"Hibbly, Hobbly, trundling hoglets,
How would you like a butt-kick by my swift pig-trotters?
Mr Popsicle took a zebra-crossing hiking route,
And got a tourist kick-shuffle straight to the curb.
He rolled himself into a prickly ball,
By a smug-looking hedgehog-hating maniac biker
Zip it hoglets, or you'll be next."

A R Trent/L A Williams

Scamp squeals. 'Rude! There's no need for that tone.'
Skipper rasps. 'Oh. Yeah! You don't scare me! And that black cat, Springer, could do with a plumpy bottom budge out of the way. Huh. She's hogging the queue as well!'
Scamp stomps. 'We won't get first dibs on the Springusaurus now. Can someone tell that stupid goose? You're not supposed to waddle on the top. You must splish-splash or slide *inside* the Springusaurus!'
Charlie purrs. 'Springer! Give that waddle-butt a meowing off!'

Springer makes a catty remark. 'Why me?'

Charlie hisses. 'Springer, we all know you can meow the loudest spit-pitch.'

Scamp shouts. 'Oye! Ducky! You can be fierce. Give that goose a palmate-foot shove. He's another one holding up the queue!'

Ducky quacks. 'I have the most delicate palmate feet. I've just given a nudge to the guinea pigs, Stanley and Steven. Okay! Just this one time, your wish is my command. This queue is so tiring.'

Little Bro and Ed were still reeling with excitement from the oasis. They launch themselves up the Springusaurus, still wearing their wetsuits.

Little Bro shouts. 'Grab that surfboard, pull it up first, then get it underneath your feet. Let's both jump on and smoothly surf downwards.'

Ed screams. 'Am I really hurtling down a swirling waterfall from side-to-side, steadying my feet on a surfboard?'

Scotty hollers. 'It's splish-splash belly-flop time!'

Ed laughs. 'The Recyclosaurus and Springusaurus are singing and chanting. They are drumming and thrusting up their tails together. Gosh! Their clunky feet thud like falling mountain rocks.'

Little Bro laughs. 'Let's rocket off the Springusaurus as if we are going up into space.'

Scotty belts out a side-splitting laugh. 'Watch me! Look at my bouncing belly-flops. I can even hop-skip-and-jump through the Springusaurus!'

Greg chuckles. 'Your Glengarry bonnet is totally drenched.'

Scotty chortles. 'Aye! It blew off my eggy-head. Our birds are entertaining themselves with Scotty's soggy find-and-fetch Glengarry bonnet.'

Ed tumbles. 'Oh! No! I'm going to make a somersault landing, belly down on top of the Springusaurus' head!'

Little Bro squeals. 'So am I! Emee, how did you end up hanging onto the Springusaurus' arm?'

Ed gasps. 'If you don't get yourself down, you'll end up taking a dive and doggy-paddle.'

Emee pants. 'Get me off!'

Crowlip tweets. 'Lady Mutt, the ultimate doggy doofus! Your kangaroo jumps are kind of useless right now!'

Bionca heckles. 'Look at them synchronising drumming tails, banging their clunky-butts and bumping scaley dome-heads. The Recyclosaurus is making a rubble-shuffle body jolt. The Springusaurus is doing a jiggle-wiggle body jerk. Good stuff! I didn't know they could stomp their feet and skid into a frenzy jiving mode..'

Professor MicroChip chuckles. 'Look what you two have done! You have woken the rainbow glowworms and seashells. They are now emerging out of the water like a display of dazzling shooting fireworks whirling around us.'

Little Bro cups his eyes. 'Not now, Recyclosaurus and Springusaurus. Don't make the three hi-fives, salute and spits.'

Ed yells. 'Did you just see that!'

Little Bro nudges Ed. 'Remember?'

Ed whispers. 'I know, nothing.'

Professor MicroChip chuckles. 'Recyclosaurus and Springusaurus are ecowarriors just like the rest of us. They deserve to have some fun too and a good spring-cleaning.'

Ed gripes. 'I'm so hungry.'

Bionca replies. 'Mm. Patience Ed.'

SECRET GARDEN FEAST

Stag gallops. 'Sweet delicious acorn pellets from the cedar trees. Thank you, grandma for my munches of woody brows, green leafy brows, bushes and shrubs.'

Grandma beckons. 'Come here you. I know your homes have disappeared and you've been sleeping rough in the humans' front gardens.'

Monty Muntjac weeps. 'There are some nice humans out there who let us sleep on their lawns. But when we munch on their garden root shrubs, they run us out because they think we are ruining their beautiful landscape gardens. We have nowhere to go. Our natural woodlands have vanished into thin air. We see new homes now, but not for us.'

Grandma EggBanger reassures. 'You will always have a home here.'

Finches flock. 'Yippee! Yummy! We're just popping by for a spot of protein-diet supper.'

Nelly perches. 'Me too, grandma.'

Grandma utters. 'I heard Nasty Patsy was up to her bullying again. Let's hope we've seen the last of her. Rumour has it, she has cubs now. She had left her cubs to hunt for food.'

Nelly squawks. 'Oh! No! She will be hunting me for cub food.'

Magpies chatter. 'We settled the score with gangster Patsy today. She lunged for the furthest foxhole and rammed her foxy-butt inside with her digging claws.'

Nelly tweets. 'I know she'll be wanting me for her cub food now.'

Perpetua replies. 'Patsy? A mother? How did she manage that! Who would fancy her? She's so nasty.'

Grandma EggBanger reassures. 'All you lovely birds have treats in store. I've prepared a hanging pick-and-mix filler. There's a scrumptious variety of seeds, nuts and grains, including sunflower heart seeds because I love you all. We have pinhead oats and pinworms. There are fatty oily suet balls so you can gain weight and stay warm if the weather regulates itself and turns back into a wintry season. But I can't feel that at the moment. But you can all enjoy the plentiful treats. The gardens are full of your favourite cherries and all kinds of berries.'

Froglips croaks. 'Grandma, what about me?'

Grandma answers. 'Oh. Froglips. I know your lilypond has turned into a stack of metal tins, batteries, screws and wire mesh. These ponds are full of bugs and algae plants.'

Nelly stammers. 'Oh. Froglips. Try not to eat the cute tiny tadpoles.'

Froglips retorts. 'We carnivores can be partial to small bugs and fishes and I'm afraid to say, if my belly rumbles any more, I'll be forced to eat smaller frogs, snails, ants, bees, beetles, cockroaches and grasshoppers.'

Nelly implores. 'Stop being nasty!'

Froglips answers. 'I will settle for clickety-click screeching stick-crickets, because they're getting on my nerves.'

Skipper and Scamp stumble. 'Hullo grandma, have you got anything for us to chomp on?'

Jax snorts. 'Hm. Might I say, not so brusque now, are you, hoglets?'

Grandma chortles. 'I know you hedgehogs feast on animal proteins. There is more than enough to go round.'

Scamp chomps. 'Num. Num. Look at those butterfly shrubs.'

Grandma replies. 'Be careful not to upset the butterfly gardens. Our Red Admirals are having a munch on the buddleia bushes. You can smell the nectar source from the blooms and honey scents.'

Skipper peers. 'I've got my eyes on that crocus buddleia sugar plum in that sunny spot.'

Scamp rejoices. 'I'm going to zonk out on those sweet red and purple arching branches.'

Masculus pesters. 'What about me?'

Grandma sighs. 'Dear Masculus. You'd eat almost anything.'

Masculus replies. 'Grandma, I can be a little pernickety at times.'

Pansy honks. 'Huh! A food-faddy you're not! You, dive into freshly baked custard tarts.'

Masculus whines. 'Go and nibble on a kibble corn, you snitch face!'

Grandma giggles. 'Pansy, I have lots of fresh water and egg-white pellets too.'

Digby oinks. 'We've been in a kerfuffle today. We are very hungry too.'

Jax complains. 'We didn't want to be food. We ran away from Suzy's thirteenth birthday sausage party bash.'

Grandma affirms. 'You're safe now. We have mixed ingredient milk foods to suit your tastebuds: eighty-percent corn, seventeen-percent soya beans and all the vitamin nutrients you need.'

Jax cheers. 'Oink! Oink! Good, stuff!'

MissRed grumbles. 'I can't eat anything.'

Grandma smiles. 'Dear MissRed, there must be something you can eat?'

MissRed whinges. 'Look at my black oil-slick makeup, my jawline is snaggled with wires. My beautiful lips are ruined!'

Grandma reassures. 'I'll try to unsnag some more of those deadly metals.'

MissRed chomps. 'Oh. Thank you, grandma. Lars has been a good help today.'

Pansy yawns. 'Ugh! He's been swooning all day over that damsel in distress, hot sea-shell on legs."

Grandma says. 'I know sea turtles are vegetarians. I have seagrass algae and sea urchins.'

MissRed replies. 'I can't see very well but they smell delicious.'

Skipper moots. 'We struggle with seeing. We nearly ate a whole plastic bag. It smelt like fresh food. It was flouncing in the waters like a jelly fish. Argh!'

Robby cheers. 'Nay! There's plenty of rabbit food dips and delicious pellets. It has carrots, lettuce, strawberries, fresh flower petals and dandelions.'

Nay twirls. 'Woo! Delicious meta organic grass and docks.'

Professor MicroChip confirms. 'Oh yes – *Rumex Crispus*.'

Grandma chuckles. 'Oops. Let's not forget there are all kinds of docks. I know your favourites are curly dock and yellow dock perennial flowering plants.'

Nay chants. 'Hooray!'

Grandma reminds. 'Robby, I haven't forgotten your dyer's woad.'

Professor MicroChip affirms. 'Yes indeed. It's the *Isatis tinctoria*. Don't worry, it won't turn your lips or teeth blue and it's safe to eat. Don't forget your favourite carrot and cotton candy–floss specials. Grandma and her helpers have been very busy preparing ecowarrior foods.'

CASTLE HUT DINER

Grandma EggBanger notices. 'EggBangers, start making your way to the food hut. Ed Williams, I think your trouser britches need a little stitching.'

Ed replies. 'Erm. Oh. Yes please, grandma EggBanger.'

Little Bro teases. 'Whip them off lad!'

Ed larks. 'Roger that, Bruv. Remember, my lips are sealed. An oath, is an oath.'

Little Bro giggles. 'Can you hear my tummy rumbling for food.'

Ed replies. 'Yes, mine too. Why didn't grandma EggBanger feed us?'

Little Bro answers. 'We get our food from the little wooden hut.'

Ed gasps. 'A real wooden hut? You mean an actual shed?'

Little Bro points. 'It's over there!'

Ed shrugs. 'An eroded wooden shack! I think I'm ready to go home now. I'll say my goodbyes to Emee before she goes to the Dog Rescue Centre.'

Little Bro chortles. 'Shush your piehole and walk with me, Bruv.'

Ed answers. 'Do I have to?'

Little Bro beckons. 'Stop dragging your feet. Look at the cranky splintery gate.'

Emee drudges. 'Anywhere is better than here.'

Little Bro laughs. 'Emee? I see you've stopped wagging your tail and your ears are now pinned back.'

Emee sniffs. 'There's nothing here worth nibbling on.'

Little Bro taunts. 'I'll open the cranky gate first.'

Ed yells. 'Sweet! Kar-azee Awesome! 'What is this?'

Little Bro beams. 'Walk with me.'

Ed chants. 'There's a cool inviting breeze around my neck. Why are the leaves on the trees smiling. Am I dreaming?'

Little Bro guides. 'We are entering another portal. Just like the Secret Garden's invisible gates.'

Ed asks. 'What is this?'

Little Bro answers. 'In plain sight, floating fluffy clouds made from sweet candy floss bubbles.'

Ed blinks. 'Sweet! Nice one! It's not just any scruffy buffy run-down hut, is it?'

Little Bro clarifies. 'It's not just any café diner. It's a magical Castle Hut Diner. An extravaganza breath-taking eatery of wishing foods. Please note: "No sick-bags allowed" so don't ask.'

Emee pants. 'More kibbles and doggy treats for me!'

Crowlip perches on a chandelier. 'I was here first. I want my wish nuts, Lady Mutt!'

Emee barks. 'Look! I have limitless crunchy treats!'

Crowlip squawks, 'You'll need a doggy-sick-bag and a poop-bag!'

Crowlip tweets. 'I don't have to share my ham-and-cheese-pickle sandwich with you anymore.'

Little Bro nudges. 'Go to the wishing-food counter; your wish will be granted.'

Scotty shouts. 'Aye wee laddie, just do it!'

Ed wishes. 'Erm. Well. I wish for: two strawberry and chocolate milk shakes, two chocolate puddings with chocolate custard. And, Erm, two triple-cheese burgers with double French fries with some squirty tomato sauce. Some more desserts: chocolate waffle cone ice-cream with peanut toppings and rainbow sprinkles. Followed by an extra-large carton of fizzy pop please. Oh and a hotdog with chilli-sauce. Thank you very much wishing-food counter.'

Greg warns. 'No extra-large sick-bags available. And no Plan B, bags up for grabs at the Castle Hut Diner!'

Bionca chants. 'Yummy! Sprouting moon-face gooey cookies and cream with jellybeans.'

Scotty clicks his tongue. 'Aye. Dab in wee laddie. You'll be home soon.'

Professor MicroChip adds. 'I need to make that important call to the Dog Rescue Centre.'

Emee blinks. 'Yikes!'

Bionca giggles. 'Ed! Your tummy is bulging. Are you sure you don't need a sick-bag?'

Greg exhibits. 'Try one of my spare Plan B bags, if you're desperate, Ed.'

Ed burps. 'Nope, I'm fine. No need for any bag assistance, thank you very much.'

Greg sniggers. 'Hahaha. I know for sure these Plan B, spacious bags work. Just ask a wandering befuddled tourist. You might spot them trying to track down those lost property areas.'

Professor MicroChip expresses. 'We have come to the end of our Castle Hut Diner feast. It is time to make our way back. Ed and Emee need to be somewhere else right now.'

Little Bro fusses. 'Ed, are you okay. You seem to be wobbling and farting at the same time.'

Ed replies. 'Just having an adventure of a life-time, that's all. Thanks for asking.'

THE RETURN OF THE DOG CATCHER!

Grandma smiles. 'What an eventful adventure for both Ed and Emee.' Professor MicroChip announces. 'I have been in contact with the Dog Rescue Centre.'

The dog catcher pulls up. 'Mm. I recognise this one. I must check her ownership status.'

Little Bro whispers. 'Come on Crowlip, let's hide in the bushes to catch a glimpse. Ed mustn't see me. Gosh! He has his hands in his left pocket and he's pulling out the crystal Tiger's eye nugget, I planted in his pocket.'

Crowlip tweets. 'I don't have to hide. You do, Little Bro. You're a secret; I'm not. Anyway, soon he won't remember you.'

Little Bro looks grim. 'I know the rules. The time-tunnel adventure will fade and he will get back to his normal life now, with Emee.'

Crowlip clicks. 'And, me.'

Ed mutters. 'Little Bro?'

Little Bro looks. 'He's whispering my name.'

The dog warden chats. 'Come on Emee. Good girl just pop yourself into the back of my white van.'

Grandad scolds. 'Ed! Where have you been? I know school closed early today. You have some explaining to do, my lad!'

Emee yaps. 'Mm. Ed's grandad really does have a humming electric car.'

Grandad puckers. 'Don't think for one minute that you are taking this mutt home with you lad! By-gum lad, you are in enough trouble!'

Ed whispers. 'Not so, kar-azee awesome.'

Crowlip squawks. 'Listen to that doofus boy!'

Little Bro hushes. 'Listen.'

Grandad blinks. 'Lou-Lou?'

Ed notices. 'Emee? Stop taking slow motion back steps. Your ears are pinned back and your tail is underneath your tummy. You know it's time to go.'

Grandad whispers. 'Emee-Lou? It's Grandad – remember me? Shh. Shh. Little pumpkin head.'

Ed shouts. 'Her tail is emerging from underneath her. She's ready for take-off like a helicopter propeller.'

Emee woofs. 'It's my lullaby, you're the kind man. I remember that smell! You're wearing your smelly house slippers!'

Ed gasps. 'Ugh! Grandad's slippers always smell like that.'

Emee whimpers. 'It's me, your pumpkin head.'

Ed whispers. 'Grandad why have you fallen to your knees with your arms flung open? Emee, what's with your famous kangaroo jumps right now?'

Grandad asserts. 'Emee-Lou was our puppy when she was just ten-weeks old. She was dognapped when you were just a little boy. She vanished and we never saw her again, until now.'

The dog catcher treads with caution. Grandad explains the whole story. Emee accompanies the dog catcher to the Dog Rescue Centre to be rehomed the legal way. He explains, the proper way is the only way to get Emee back. There are no legal documents to show so grandad has no rights to Emee.

Ed mopes. 'Oh. Emee. You won't be fighting over my ham-and-cheese-pickle sandwich anymore.'

The dog catcher warns. 'The law says you cannot take Emee home with you.'

Grandad implores. 'Can you check her chip identification to see if the dog-napper bothered to change her records?'

Ed puckers. 'That is the law; do your checks.'

The dog warden makes investigations by phone. Ed and grandad listen. 'Oh! When? A runaway scruffy stray thinks that she's a dog-escapologist? Loves the local tram stops? Countless reports of missing by Mr Williams? Mm. Everything seems correct this side. She looks happy and healthy. It sounds like a fairy tale ending.'

The dog warden steps out of the van still clutching onto the loop around Emee's neck. The dog warden walks towards grandad.

He affirms. 'Mr Williams, I believe Emee-Lou belongs to you and your grandson.'

Grandad whispers. 'Emee-Lou, pumpkin-head, it's me, grandad.'

Emee recalls. 'Woof! Woof! Roll over, wag tail in propeller mode, shuffle on the floor, stick slavery tongue out and look cute. Then, wait for the tickly belly-rubs.'

Emee yaps:

"The dog-napper flitted me away, that's how I ended up as a runaway stray.

He wouldn't flash the cash to say: 'I'm worth it.'

I fled the clutches of the evil dog snatcher, to a friendly dog catcher.

No longer kept in a cold cellar, my tail wags like helicopter propellers.

I'll never be a waif because I'm safe.

No need to use my sniffer nozzle for scraps at the local tram-stops.

That green-snot-drip, school-gate crow is fluttering by for a visit.

Crowlip tweets: 'I'm not sharing my ham-and-cheese-pickle sandwich with Lady Mutt."

Emee says: I'll have my own bed and swanky blanky with my own snuggle ruffle duvet, with lots of belly rubs.

I can briskly kangaroo jump, but no longer a blockbuster dog-escapologist disaster.

I, Emee-Lou Williams am reunited with my happily ever-after."

A R Trent

PROFESSOR MICROCHIP CONCLUDES

LA-LA Forest Park's eventful ecowarrior mission was successful. The migration birds and MissRed were safely guided home.

The nocturnal wildlife keeps a watchful eye whilst the rest lie napping, nestling, snuggling and burrowing. Masculus takes a permanent residency in the Secret Garden. He insists on a fitted digital door-buzzer that switches off. And, a 'DO NOT DISTURB' sign, so that he get's lots of snoozes.

Professor MicroChip gives a huge sigh. He gazes up at the dark clouds of the natural ionised gases putting on the most dazzling displays in the universe, deep in thought.

Handsome, Blute and BirdCop perch close by. 'Another successful ecowarrior campaign today.'

The Prof concludes. 'Let's keep it serene. Recyclosaurus and Springusaurus, you did another excellent job today.'

Blute asks. 'I wonder what Ed is doing now?'

Prof answers. 'Ed met his future unborn. The two worlds collided in a little boy's dream, a quantum-leap time-travel. He will wake up tomorrow morning and remember nothing about the Secret Garden or even meeting EggBangers or ecowarriors. Ed will recall his memorable dream someday about getting himself lost and the day he got reunited with Emee-Lou. And the crow that perches on his school gates, waiting for food scraps, will become a familiar joyful yet annoying sight. He will complete his interesting climate-change project and attain full marks.'

The EggBangers say. 'Climate change affects us all. It is a non-progressive attacker. The backlash will be a mammoth task for the unborn.'

Professor MicroChip concludes. 'Peak into the future of the unborn historians a few hundred years from now, they may think: our ancestors pledges didn't go far enough. Look what they've done to us!'